GW01316263

TRAILS TO
FREEDOM

TRAILS TO
FREEDOM

THE TRUE STORY OF THE MEDIEVAL TRAILS USED BY
ANZAC POWS TO ESCAPE ITALY IN 1943–1944

SIMON TANCRED

Hardie Grant

BOOKS

Published in 2025 by Hardie Grant Books,
an imprint of Hardie Grant Publishing

Hardie Grant Books (Melbourne)
Wurundjeri Country
Level 11, 36 Wellington Street
Collingwood, Victoria 3066

Hardie Grant North America
2912 Telegraph Ave
Berkeley, California 94705

hardiegrant.com/books

Hardie Grant acknowledges the Traditional
Owners of the Country on which we work,
the Wurundjeri People of the Kulin Nation
and the Gadigal People of the Eora Nation,
and recognises their continuing connection
to the land, waters and culture. We pay our
respects to their Elders past and present.

All rights reserved. No part of this
publication may be reproduced, stored in
a retrieval system or transmitted in any
form by any means, electronic, mechanical,
photocopying, recording or otherwise,
without the prior written permission of the
publishers and copyright holders.

The moral rights of the author have been
asserted.

Copyright text © Simon Tancred 2025

A catalogue record for this
book is available from the
National Library of Australia

Trails to Freedom
ISBN 978 1 76145 175 1
ISBN 978 1 76144 314 5 (ebook)

10 9 8 7 6 5 4 3 2 1

Publishing Director: Pam Brewster
Commissioning Editor: Claire Davis
Head of Editorial: Jasmin Chua
Editor: Nadine Davidoff
Creative Director: Kristin Thomas
Designer: Kate Barraclough
Head of Production: Todd Rechner
Production Controller: Jessica Harvie

Cover image (top) courtesy of the
family of Carl Alexander Carrigan.
Left to right: Carl Carrigan, Paul
Carrigan and Ron Fitzgerald.

Back cover image of John Fairfax
Tancred courtesy of the family of
Simon Tancred.

Printed in Australia by Griffin Press,
an Accredited ISO AS/NZS 14001
Environmental Management System
printer.

The paper this book is printed
on is certified against the Forest
Stewardship Council® Standards.
Griffin Press holds FSC® chain
of custody certification SCS-
COC-001185. FSC® promotes
environmentally responsible, socially
beneficial and economically viable
management of the world's forests.

For Carolyn, Grace and Peter,
with all my love

CONTENTS

PROLOGUE 9

CHAPTER 1 13

CHAPTER 2 43

CHAPTER 3 79

CHAPTER 4 113

CHAPTER 5 153

CHAPTER 6 187

CHAPTER 7 215

CHAPTER 8 257

CHAPTER 9 269

AFTERWORD 283

ACKNOWLEDGEMENTS 286

READING LIST 287

MAP OF THE WALKING TRAIL

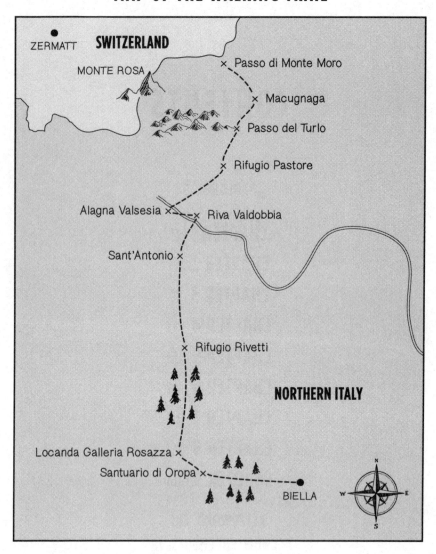

ZERMATT
SWITZERLAND
MONTE ROSA
× Passo di Monte Moro
× Macugnaga
× Passo del Turlo
× Rifugio Pastore
Alagna Valsesia × × Riva Valdobbia
Sant'Antonio ×
× Rifugio Rivetti
NORTHERN ITALY
Locanda Galleria Rosazza ×
Santuario di Oropa ×
BIELLA

LOCATION OF TRAIL
IN ITALY

-- TRAIL
× STOPS ON THE ROUTE
● NEARBY CITIES/TOWNS
= SESIA RIVER
— BORDER BETWEEN ITALY AND SWITZERLAND

PROLOGUE

With her arms outstretched against the pale blue sky, the golden Madonna seems to beckon, calling me towards her. She looks over my shoulder towards the splendour of the north face of Monte Rosa, Europe's second-highest peak, which sits like a sleeping giant on the other side of the deep valley. I grab the chain with both hands, dig the caps of my boots into snow and haul myself up to where she stands on a granite plinth marking the Monte Moro Pass, the border between Italy and Switzerland.

Seven days ago I began my hike in Biella, a prosperous textile town 95 kilometres north of Turin, where the Po River plain butts up against the foothills of the Italian Alps. I started walking in sweltering heat and now I'm finishing in knee-deep snow. I've walked over 100 kilometres down three valleys and across five passes, and climbed over 5000 metres. I've survived an electrical storm, torrential rain, a snow squall and three falls, and been lost only twice.

I slide off my pack, rest it on the snow, and then peel off my gloves and shove them into my back pocket. A small, laminated photo is dangling from a carabiner on the side of my pack – a black-and-white portrait of a handsome young man with dark hair and a crooked smile. He's wearing a slouch hat and looking directly into the camera. I unclip the photograph, climb up the plinth and sit on a cold stone step, my back against the statue. I take a handkerchief out of my pocket, wipe the picture and stand it up in the snow beside me, adjusting it so that he can enjoy the view as well.

I unzip my jacket and take out a small packet of Drum tobacco. I tear off the plastic, stow it in an outer pocket and slide my finger under the seal. Holding the packet to my nose, I breathe in the sweet smell, then I take out a thin white packet of papers. I pull out one of the gummed sheets and stick it on the edge of my lip. The tobacco in the pouch is fine and moist, and I work a small plug in the palm of my hand, stretching it lengthways. Then I put the two together and roll a perfect cigarette. My dexterity surprises me; I haven't done this for many years. I take a plastic lighter out of my inner pocket, cup my hands against the wind and, after three attempts, light the cigarette. The empty end flares like a candle. I wave away the ash and pull on the cigarette, inhaling deeply before dissolving into a fit of coughing. Once I've recovered, I lean back against the wall and look at the photo, waving the cigarette aloft.

'There you go, Uncle John. We made it!' I take another, more cautious, drag on the cigarette and slowly exhale. A smoke ring wobbles towards Monte Rosa before dissipating in the light breeze. 'Not bad, eh?'

I now hate smoking. But Uncle John always enjoyed it. When I inherited his gramophone, the needle box was full of ancient cigarette butts. I have another photo of him standing in a stockyard, hands on his hips, a cheeky smile on his face and a dhurrie hanging from his lip.

I stub the cigarette out in the snow and put it inside the plastic wrapping in my pocket, then I slip the photo of Uncle John in beside the tobacco.

With cautious movements, I work my way around to the northern side of the plinth. Pressed against the stone and wary of the ice, I set myself against the wall and look down into the Saastal, the deep glacial valley leading into the heart of Switzerland. Even in the snow I can make out a squiggly line like a balloon string: a trail that leads down from the pass, runs along the edge of a long blue lake and disappears. Between September 1943 and March 1944, several hundred Australian and New Zealand ex-prisoners of war used this trail to escape Italy and find freedom in neutral Switzerland. My uncle John Fairfax Tancred was not one of them.

I never knew John. A volunteer in the Australian Imperial Forces (AIF), fighting for king and country against Nazi Germany and Fascist Italy, he died a terrible death in the blue waters of the Mediterranean, off the coast of the Peloponnese in 1941. He was a young, single man with no children. I am probably, surely, the only person alive who has given him a second thought or even knows who he was. He deserved a better end.

John was one of millions of young men and women whose lives were squandered in those years. He was a volunteer who chose to go to war on the other side of the world – probably for the adventure that it promised but also with a sense of duty, to do his bit protecting Australia and the British empire from Germany and its allies. I had never known how to honour his memory until an idea fell into my lap that transformed me.

CHAPTER 1

The *sentieri della libertà* have existed for hundreds of years. A network of trails crisscrossing the mountains between Oropa and Valsesia in northern Italy, they've been used since at least the Middle Ages, probably much earlier. They served as pilgrim routes connecting the valley communities with sacred sites; trade routes for merchants bearing goods from the Valsesia over the mountains and into neighbouring Gressoney, once considered part of France; and migration routes carrying people from Switzerland into the valleys of Piedmont and Aosta. Even in the most remote parts of the mountains, droving trails are scored into the land, used by local shepherds and cowherds to move their animals up to the high summer pastures and back. At the height of World

War II, this grid of interweaving and overlapping paths far from Fascist patrols served the resistance, who used them to communicate with their leaders, many of whom had found refuge in neutral Switzerland. It was during this time, when they were also used by escaping Allied POWs and refugees seeking safety, that this random network of donkey tracks and mule trails was christened with the name *sentieri della libertà,* the trails to freedom.

The mountain trails fell into disuse after the end of World War II. Many of the small, isolated mountain settlements were abandoned, whole communities drawn to the opportunities offered by the newly industrialised cities on the plains. Flocks and herds began to be moved by trucks. In the 1980s, the Club Alpino Italiano (CAI) started to reopen the trails for recreational use. The mountains were being rediscovered not as places of work and endeavour but as places to escape from the grinding lifestyle of the big cities, re-establishing connections with a simpler way of life that seemed to be disappearing. In the summer months, volunteers trekked up into the mountains to establish *rifugi* in the forsaken shepherds' huts, providing shelter for hikers looking for a place to overnight. These simple mountain lodges offered beds, usually bunks in dormitories; and somewhere to eat, robust local food shared at a common table. Many of the paths were strung together to create long-distance, multi-day trails that took the hikers through some of the most magnificent country in the Alps: soaring snow-capped mountains, glaciers, deep lakes, primeval forests and deep green valleys scattered with isolated hamlets and villages.

It wasn't my uncle John's story that led me to these trails. At least, not at first. It was the story of another Australian soldier who also grew up in the bush, not so far from where John was raised. His name was Carl Carrigan. The two men never met, that I know of, but they had a lot in common. They were more or less the same age. John was born in 1912, Carl was born in 1913; Carl was raised on a sheep property out of Moree, New South Wales, while Uncle John was raised on a cattle property near Dalby, 200 kilometres north over the Queensland border. They both enlisted in June 1940 and they both found themselves in North Africa in 1941, fighting the Italians with success and then the Germans with less success. Carl was in an anti-tank unit, while John was in the infantry. They both ended up being taken prisoner by the Germans, Carl in Fort Mechili near Tobruk in Libya, and John several months later at El-Alamein in Egypt. They were both handed over to the Italians to be transported to Italy, but this is where their stories diverge: Carl made it to Italy, John didn't.

After more than two years as a prisoner of war in northern Italy, Carl escaped to Switzerland in 1943 with three other men: his brother Paul Carrigan, Ron Fitzgerald and Lloyd Ledingham. They fled Italy as it was collapsing into a bitter civil war, the German-occupied north resisting the advance of the Allies in the south. To get there, they followed the *sentieri della libertà,* a one-hundred-kilometre trek that took them over some of the most forbidding terrain in the Alps. They had no guides, no maps, no food and spoke little to no Italian. They had only the clothes they were standing in when they were released, and they were passing through enemy territory. And yet, somehow, they made it. This is the story of their odyssey, but it is also the story of my uncle John.

When Cate Carrigan, Carl's daughter, first rang me up, introduced herself and asked for my help to organise a three-week holiday in Italy for eleven people, my heart sank. I had been organising walking tours in Italy for nearly thirty years. Cate was a school friend of Carolyn, my wife. Researching and shaping their holiday was going to involve a lot of work, it was a busy time and I could see that, as they were family friends, I wasn't going to make a lot of money. However, politeness prevailed and we agreed to meet.

Cate is a journalist. She became interested in documenting her father's World War II experiences when she was in her twenties but Carl, like most veterans, was reluctant to talk about his experience of the war. It was only towards the end of his life that he started to open up. Over the years, as more family members began asking questions and friends of Carl's shared their own diaries and recollections, Cate's interest grew. She eventually put together a twenty-page account of her father's war-time experiences that chronicled this: enrolment in Sydney in 1940, his training in Palestine, the fighting in the deserts of Libya, his peregrinations as a prisoner of war in Benghazi and then in central and northern Italy, and, finally, his escape to freedom in Switzerland at the end of 1943. Twenty years after Carl's death, the family decided to go to Italy to have a holiday and to visit the places where Carl had been. It was a brilliant idea and that's where I came in.

A week after our phone conversation, Cate came over to my place in Surry Hills in Sydney. She walked in with a folder full of papers and a box of freshly baked *ricciarelli* – soft Italian almond biscuits, which also happen to be my favourites. I liked her immediately.

'Would you like some coffee?' I asked.

I loaded the Moka and put it on a low gas flame. We sat down at the kitchen table, and Cate laid out some grainy black-and-white photos – holiday shots of three young men in newly pressed military fatigues, berets on their heads, leaning against a railing with soaring mountains and glaciers behind them. They were smiling, enjoying their new-found freedom.

'That's Dad and his mates in Switzerland, waiting to be sent home,' said Cate. 'Dad's in the middle, Lloyd Ledingham is on the left and Dad's brother Paul is on the right. It was pretty good in Switzerland, really. They were able to work, save some money. Dad learned how to ski while he was there.' She took another biscuit. 'Not many happy snaps from the first part of their journey, though,' she added.

Understandably, Carl hadn't dwelt on the horror of inexperienced country boys confronting the Panzer tanks of General Erwin Rommel's Afrika Corps in the Libyan desert in full summer, nor did he dwell on the humiliation and privations of being interred in a barbed-wire prison camp on the outskirts of Benghazi. Just the bare facts.

At 3.30 pm on 14 November 1940, Carl Carrigan left Wharf 9 in Pyrmont in Sydney harbour. He was bound for war aboard the *RMS Orion,* an ocean liner that belonged to the Orient Steam Navigation Company. It had been converted into a troop carrier.

It took the contingent over a month to get to their destination in Palestine. They spent three months training there before getting the call to leave for action in the western desert of Libya. Here they were to join British and Indian forces who were trying to stop the rapid advance of the Axis forces, a combination of Italian and German battalions, who were led by General Rommel, the famous 'Desert Fox'.

The Australians were ferried across the Suez Canal and then taken by train to Alexandria. From here they were trucked across the Sollum Escarpment into Libya and then driven to Tobruk. Their final destination was Mechili, a rat hole in the desert, 200 kilometres further west. They dug themselves into a holding position and waited. They didn't have to wait long.

On 6 April, Mechili was surrounded by the Axis forces and pounded by their artillery. Carl was part of an anti-tank unit. His first contact with the enemy was unexpected. They had been anticipating support from the British Second Armoured Division. When they saw tanks emerging through the morning mist, they thought it was backup, but they were horrified to discover they were actually facing German Panzer tanks.

The following day, two separate German envoys demanded the surrender of the beleaguered site but the British commanding officer, Major-General Gambier-Parry, refused. He attempted twice to break through the cordon that night and head for Tobruk, leaving the Australians and some Indian soldiers to fight a rear-guard action, but both breakouts were unsuccessful. The Allied soldiers resisted hard with their inadequate weapons, sacrificial lambs they felt, but eventually they succumbed. On the morning of 8 April, Gambier-Parry decided to surrender to avoid further casualties. Nearly 3000 British, Indian and Australian troops became prisoners under the control of Major-General Pietro Zaglio of the Italian army. After four days in the trenches, Carl and his mates' brief combat experience had come to an end.

The prisoners became the responsibility of the Italian army. They were loaded onto trucks and driven 250 kilometres across the desert to a primitive prison camp in Benghazi on the western coast of Libya. Conditions were appalling. After a week, they were taken across the sea to Italy, loaded onto unmarked ships which ran the Allied blockade. They made it safely to Naples on 7 May.

I poured the coffee and spread out a map of Italy on the kitchen table.

'You know what is really remarkable about this story?' Cate said. 'Dad, his brother Paul, Lloyd Ledingham and Ron Fitzgerald, four friends, all signed up together on the same day in Sydney in 1940. They then trained in Palestine together. They went into battle in North Africa together. They were all taken prisoner together on the same day. They went through two-and-a-half years as prisoners of war together, they escaped together and, finally, got to safety in Switzerland together. Isn't that something?'

I had to agree. 'What are the chances?'

We put our cups aside, leant over the map and began to track Carl's journey through Italy. Carl and his mates had arrived in Naples on 7 May 1941. They stayed nearby, in a camp in Capua, before being trained north to a holding camp in Sulmona, a small town in the mountains 100 kilometres east of Rome.

'They were only there for ten days, though,' said Cate. 'There were a lot of British prisoners already being held there. Mostly officers. Quite comfy. They were glad to see the rowdy colonials go.'

The Anzacs were then transferred to Bolzano, 700 kilometres north on the Austrian border. It's a beautiful town: baroque architecture, arcades, mountains all around. They were held in a camp 10 kilometres to the north, in a village overlooking the Isarco River. The camp was improvised out of an old brewery.

'Dad said it was a reasonable-enough place,' Cate told me. 'He said that the locals were quite friendly. They would ride out on the weekends to stare in at these strange prisoners through the wire. A few Sikh POWs used to unravel their uncut beards to amuse them.'

In October, as winter closed in, the prisoners were sent to a purpose-built facility: Campo 57. It was 200 kilometres to the east, on the windswept plains between Udine and the Yugoslav border, near a village called Grupignano.

The conditions in Campo 57 were terrible. The food was bad and hard to come by, and the housing was crowded and filthy. They stayed in timber huts that were poorly built and offered little protection against the bitter winter winds.

There were no doctors, and the prisoners had to improvise their own medical treatment.

'Summary executions were common,' said Cate. 'Prisoners were shot there and then, for no good reason. The commandant was a card-carrying Fascist, Colonel Vittorio Calcaterra. He was a real bastard, according to Dad. Not your standard "good Italian".'

Lloyd didn't mince his words, either. He described Calcaterra as a sadist, a beast and an accessory to murder.

'He would have been tried as a war criminal,' Cate explained, 'but the partisans got him first and executed him.' She reached for another *ricciarello.*

In April 1943, when Carl had been in Campo 57 for eighteen months, the guards asked for volunteers with farming backgrounds to help plant and bring in the crops. All the eligible Italian men were off fighting the war. Carl, his brother and their friends had reservations about supporting the enemy war effort, but they put their hands up anyway. Surely, they thought, there would be better conditions – and better chances to escape. They soon found themselves on a train heading west across northern Italy to Vercelli, a small city in the middle of the vast Po River floodplain, halfway between Milan and Turin.

The floodplain was a patchwork of fields divided by high embankments lined with rows of poplars. In the middle were scattered *cascine,* large, fortified farm complexes made up of homes, stables, barns, dairies and sometimes even schools and small churches. They were fortified in the seventeenth and eighteenth centuries, when armies and bushrangers roamed the plains unmolested. They were the perfect place to hold POW farm labourers.

It was spring when the 500 Anzac soldiers from Campo 57 arrived. The snow in the mountains was starting to melt, creating the icy waters that flowed onto the plain and were diverted into an ancient network of irrigation channels. As the fields flooded, the plain was converted into a sea of rice paddies – a vast expanse of mirrors reflecting the cloudy sky. The men were distributed among the *cascine*. Guards were allocated to each farmhouse and the prisoners' boots were confiscated each night to discourage escape. Still, the conditions were a vast improvement on Campo 57.

When Carl and his friends arrived at their *cascina,* they were issued with two blankets, two sheets, a pillow and two loaves of bread before being taken to their spotless barracks. They had to work long hours in the fields and so were fed properly. They also supplemented their diet with whatever they could find or scrounge – frogs from the rice paddies, beans, milk and eggs.

Some guards spoke English and the *padroni,* the property owners, were often sympathetic. One *padrone* joked with the prisoners, showing them photos of himself as an officer in World War I, serving as an ally of the British. The prisoners made friends with the locals and some even had affairs with local girls.

'Dad said that the prisoners refused to plant the rice,' Cate told me as we studied the map together. 'They said standing in water all day was unhealthy. Somehow, they got away with it. I don't know how that worked. So the planting was done by these young women brought up from Milan. They were called *mondine* and apparently were billeted in the same *cascine* as the POWs. That's just asking for trouble, isn't it?' She laughed. 'Dad couldn't believe it. I quote, "All these beautiful girls with their bums in the air planting the rice." Not what you want to hear from your father!'

By then, news was filtering through that things weren't going so well for the Italians. Even before the soldiers had left Campo 57, they'd heard that the Allies had retaken North Africa and pushed into southern Italy. They were now working their way up the peninsula and Italy was facing defeat. On 25 July 1943 Benito Mussolini was replaced by General Pietro Badoglio and sent into exile. Badoglio opened secret negotiations with the Allies. Then, on 3 September 1943, Italy signed an armistice with the Allies. They had switched sides. The treaty wasn't made public until five days later, on 8 September, which gave the Italian leadership – king, generals and politicians alike – time to escape to Allied-held southern Italy, leaving the Italian armies and people of German-occupied northern Italy to their fate.

'When they heard about the armistice, many of the prison guards around Vercelli laid down their arms, opened the prison gates and celebrated with the prisoners,' said Cate. 'They hugged and drank wine.'

The Fascists had led the country into a disastrous war. They had never been popular in Piedmont and by the end of 1943 they were hated. One guard told Carl that they, the POWs, had been prisoners for two years, while they, the Italian people, had been prisoners for twenty years.

Many of the guards and families around Vercelli believed the war was over but it didn't work out like that. Most of the provincial authorities stayed loyal to the Fascists and their Nazi supporters, clinging to power. The Germans themselves, who were in Italy shoring up their faulting allies, were furious. The Italians had betrayed them in World War I and now they had done so again.

The Germans had suspected that the Italians would flip sides and had been bringing in reinforcements for several months. With the help of local collaborators, the Germans moved quickly and brutally to assert control. Italy was plunged into a cruel civil war that would go on for another eighteen months, fought between those who remained loyal to Mussolini and the Germans and those who resisted, passively or actively, dreaming of a reborn Italy as they waited for the American and British forces to fight their way north.

The former POWs, Carl and his friends included, stayed on at the unguarded *cascina* for a few more days, working in the fields for their food and keep, listening to the rumours and trying to figure out a plan. The Germans had quickly taken control of towns and cities and had sent patrols out into the countryside, issuing decrees that anyone found harbouring Allied prisoners would be shot.

Only a few days after their release, the soldiers made contact with local resistance groups. Most decided it was time to leave for their own safety, and for the safety of the local people who were helping them. One stormy night, a large group, including Carl, his brother and friends, set off for the mountains and the Swiss border, led by two young local partisan officers. It was 19 September, nearly two weeks after the armistice.

Cate flipped through her notes. She had circled in pencil the places she knew Carl had touched on the way out of Italy. From Selve they moved to a farm near Arro and Vermogno and then on to the town of Biella, at the foothills of the Alps. They climbed up to the medieval sanctuary of Oropa. 'That's where the trail goes cold for a few days,' said Cate. 'The next place he mentions by name is somewhere called Sant'Antonio.'

We scanned the map and eventually found Sant'Antonio, a tiny hamlet a long way north. To get from Oropa to Sant'Antonio, they would've gone north into the neighbouring Cervo Valley and then across vast expanses of uninhabited mountains. It was a long way with some brutal climbs crossing passes, valleys and the empty ridges and peaks. It took the men three days to get over this wasteland.

From Sant'Antonio they went down into the Valsesia, the valley of the Sesia River, before turning north and walking towards the head of the valley. On the way, they passed through the last two towns of the valley, Riva Valdobbia and Alagna, which Carl remembered well because they had been given food and wine. The northern end of the Valsesia was closed off by Monte Rosa, an enormous, hunched massif, a string of peaks over 4000 metres high. In Alagna, at the foot of the mountain, the POWs learned that the path to the north skirted around the eastern side of the mountain, crossing the Passo del Turlo. At the top of the pass, the soldiers would have seen the border with Switzerland for the first time: a ridge-line in the distance. They descended into the Quarazza Valley, bypassing the village of Macugnaga, and finally climbing up to the Passo di Monte Moro, the border pass into Switzerland and freedom. They crossed over on 3 October 1943.

As Cate talked about her father's experiences in North Africa, I realised that they would have been the same as the experiences of my uncle John. I marvelled at the idea that her father and my uncle might even have known each other. They had so much in common, I'm sure that if they had met, they would have been fast friends.

After Cate left, I went upstairs and hunted around in cupboards until I found a box full of family memorabilia that my father had left me. I knew somewhere in there were photos of Uncle John. I found them in an old leather writing case. In one photo, he was sitting on the back steps of Burrandown, his family homestead in south-western Queensland, wearing moleskins and a light-coloured work shirt with the sleeves rolled up, his arms resting on his knees. He was squinting into the sun, looking at the photographer with a crooked smile. In another he was unrecognisable, a cowboy on the back of a rearing bullock, one arm waving high, the other hanging on for dear life to a belt tight around the beast's belly. In a third he was a cocky young digger smiling at the camera under his slouch hat.

Had he survived the Mediterranean crossing in August 1941, John would have ended up in Campo 57 in Grupignano and, I'm sure, given his farming background, he would have been selected to work in the rice fields around Vercelli in April 1943. I imagine too that after the armistice, he, like Carl Carrigan, would have headed to the Alps to freedom. He may even have joined Carl's crew.

I returned downstairs to the kitchen, sat down and studied the rough line I had drawn in pencil on the map as Cate spoke. It ran along ridges, passes and valleys. One hundred kilometres through the heart of the Alps. Ten days of hiking. An idea started to take shape in my mind.

My family is a bit thin on the ground. Both my grandfathers died before I met them. So did my two uncles, both called John: my father's brother John, who died in World War II; and my mother's brother John, who died in a plane crash in 1960. Both my grandmothers lived interstate, so I didn't see much of them. My mother died when I was four and we had very little to do with her side of the family while I was growing up. Losing a wife and a mother has a devastating effect on a family. My father was old-school and raised us on his own, although we did have a live-in housekeeper for the first six years or so – Mrs Mutton, a kindly, silver-haired English lady who gave me my first Bible. Dad was an eligible man, but he stayed on his own for more than twenty years. Perhaps he didn't want to introduce an unpredictable element into our already dysfunctional family. There were no photos of my mother in the house, and we rarely talked about her. It was very 'stiff upper lip and get on with things' – the way my father's generation had always dealt with the tragedies that befell them.

From what I could gather, my dad's brother John was a

knock-about kind of guy, a true Queensland bushie, at least on the surface. While I was growing up, he assumed a mythical quality for me, becoming part of my strategy to combat the loneliness at night: my imaginary cowboy uncle who lived with an imaginary family in a rambling homestead in south-western Queensland. That I shared his middle name, Fairfax, helped this conceit. I'd fantasise about going to visit them, the long drive north, windows down to combat the stinking heat, staying for a chaotic, dusty Christmas. My father told me that John had taught him how to ride and how to shoot before he was seven. When my father was a year older, John started taking him out overnight with the droving team – my eight-year-old dad on his own horse with his own rifle. I wanted a slice of that.

When my grandfather died of pneumonia in 1934, aged fifty-nine, he left behind my grandmother Daisy; John, who was aged twenty-two; and my father, Peter, who was aged fifteen. John was the heir apparent and helped to manage the family's 5000-acre property after his father's death. My father was more academic than his brother. He saw the war coming, gave up his plans to become a journalist or a vet, and signed up for officer training at the Royal Military College of Duntroon in Canberra. John, on the other hand, bided his time. He enlisted as a regular soldier in the infantry in June 1940, the same as Carl and his friends. Despite his role as a manager of a large family property, John described his occupation as 'station hand', I imagine because he didn't want any favours or special treatment.

He started as a private and was quickly promoted to a corporal. He left Sydney on 27 December 1940, bound for North Africa, and arrived in Ismailia on the Suez Canal on 30 January 1941. In scribbly writing crammed on a single line, his service record notes that one month after arriving on 22 February in Khassa, a training camp in Palestine, John went AWOL for forty-two hours and thirty minutes. I have no idea what he got up to, no other details were provided and none of the letters he wrote home survive; I imagine it wasn't the kind of thing you would want to share with your mother anyway. I do hope he had a high old time though, as it was his last opportunity to have some fun. As a result of this indiscretion, he forfeited two days' pay and was reduced to private again. He was quickly promoted once more and then just as quickly demoted, this time for insolence to an officer. When I discovered this, I liked him even more.

In early April 1941, his battalion, the 2/32nd, joined the fighting in the western desert. The first battle of El-Alamein started on 22 July when Allied forces tried to stop the ever-advancing German Panzers. The 2/32nd suffered heavily. Nearly half its number were either killed or wounded and nearly 200, including Uncle John, became prisoners of war.

As happened to Carl, the Germans handed John and his fellow prisoners over to the Italians in Benghazi for processing.

The conditions were appalling. The compound in Benghazi was 50 metres wide, 350 metres long and surrounded by barbed wire. It held between 3000 and 4000 men. The regime was harsh with cruel public punishments meted out summarily. It was the middle of the North African summer and there was no shelter, apart from a couple of tall date trees, which gave the compound its nickname: the Palms.

The men slept in the open. Some had ground sheets that also served as makeshift tents, but most simply lay down in the dirt wherever they could find a spot. Dysentery was rife. An open pit straddled by a long pole to perch on served as the latrine. More than one ill soldier lost his balance and fell in. Food was scarce and poor quality. The daily rations were 100 grams of tinned meat (probably horse meat), 200 grams of bread, a cup of rice soup and a cup of ersatz coffee (probably acorn meal).

Less than a month later, on 16 August 1943, the Allied troops were marched from the Palms to the port of Benghazi where two converted cargo ships waited: the *Sestriere* and the *Nino Bixio*. The POWs were divided alphabetically by surname: A to L boarded the *Sestriere* and M to Z boarded the *Nino Bixio*, including Private John Tancred. The *Nino Bixio* was a modern ship – it had only been launched a year earlier in Genoa – but the conditions in the holds, where nearly 3000 POWs were forced to go, were primitive. The two ships sailed for Brindisi in southern Italy, escorted by the destroyers *Saetta* and *Nicoloso da Recco* and the torpedo boats *Castore* and *Orione*.

The following afternoon, 17 August, the *Nino Bixio* was stalked by the *Turbulent,* a British submarine tasked with patrolling the Mediterranean to disrupt enemy shipping. Somehow the *Turbulent's* captain, 'Tubby' Linton, who was considered one of the Royal Navy's greatest submarine commanders, was able to avoid the ship's escort and, at exactly 15.35 Italian time, sent off three torpedoes, two of which hit the *Nino Bixio* with colossal violence, tearing holes in the forward hold where nearly 300 men were packed in darkness and silence. It was a horror show. Over 200 men died, including 116 New Zealanders and forty-one Australians. Many of those who weren't killed instantly by the explosions were drowned, men and debris being sucked in and out of the jagged holes as the water surged. Around thirty more men were seriously injured and, miraculously, around thirty men survived unhurt. Unfortunately, my uncle John wasn't one of these.

Through luck and the remarkable seamanship of the Italian captain, Antonio Raggio, and his crew, the *Nino Bixio* was able to make it to port at Navarino in Greece. Raggio was later given the Bronze Medal by the Italian Navy for his valour and competence. He was highly regarded by the survivors for the humanity and courage he showed on that day. After the end of the war, the *Nino Bixio* was converted and re-entered service as a freighter in 1952. On 8 January 1955, the *Nino Bixio* arrived at the port of Napier in New Zealand to deliver goods from Italy. It did not go unobserved. At its next stop, a small ceremony, involving the then captain, Enrico Sambolino, and a number of survivors, was held to commemorate the events of August 1943. Antonio Raggio died in 1959, aged fifty-five. In 1992, his son Cesare was invited to New Zealand as a guest of the survivors' association to commemorate the fiftieth anniversary of the attack.

After months of being classified as 'missing in action' and then as a prisoner of war, John was finally declared 'killed in action'. His body was never retrieved. He is commemorated by name on the Alamein Memorial at El-Alamein, Column 94.

My grandmother, John's mother, was a widow living on a large cattle property by herself, her two sons overseas fighting in the war – one in North Africa and one in New Guinea. I still have the flimsy telegram that informed her of John's death.

The details of the torpedoing of the *Nino Bixio* remained a mystery for many years. Captain Tubby Linton was a national hero. The *Turbulent* was finally sunk in 1943 and Linton was awarded a posthumous Victoria Cross. The *Nino Bixio* was flying neither the Red Cross nor a white flag. There was no cover-up – bad things happen in war – but the tragedy seemed to disappear from the records. It was only three years before his own death that my father learned the full details of his brother's death.

In January 1990, my father wrote a brief biography of John for a local history project. 'John,' he wrote, 'was a hardworking, conscientious young man who was loved and respected by his community. He was not a natural scholar, nor did he excel in organised sports, but he enjoyed his time at school and was a popular member of the school fraternity. He was also an active member of his local Kingaroy community. He was a committee member of the Burrandown Picnic Races Club and regularly played competition tennis.' He concluded by saying: 'He was a talented bushman and an excellent horseman. In his free time he enjoyed dancing and was a keen participant in the local agricultural shows, taking part in, and often winning, the camp-drafting, tent pegging and bullock riding.'

The last images I have of John do not tally with this young man. They are held by the Australian War Memorial in Canberra, the official photos taken when he enlisted: a frontal photo and a profile. More mugshots than portraits, the new soldier in these photos is a country mile from the confident bushy sitting on the back step of the family homestead. He is wearing a loose-fitting woollen tunic with epaulets and two pleated breast pockets that seems a size or two too big. He's clean-shaven and has freshly cut, close-cropped hair. There is a sadness about him. He is staring into the camera with resignation as if he has intimations of his mortality.

~‿⁓

The story of Carl's escape had captivated me but it was the connection with my late uncle that really sealed the deal. It was a gift, an invitation to explore the gnarly, glacier-scoured ranges of Italy's western Alps, so different from the filigree limestone pinnacles and green valleys of the Dolomites in the eastern Alps that I already knew well through my tours. I was inspired by the resilience of these young Aussies lost in a foreign land and I was moved by the courage and graciousness of the people who helped them along the way. I really had to walk that trail too. It was a way of honouring the sacrifices that these young men had made and it was a way of honouring my uncle as well. I started planning, and the first thing I needed was some maps.

The heavy cardboard tube was waiting for me when I got home from the office. It had been hand-delivered to my front door by registered mail a month after I had placed my order. I was very excited. I made myself a cup of tea then went upstairs, tube under my arm. I popped the plastic lid, slid the scroll out, rolling the thick pages in reverse and spreading them out, one by one, on my desk, using stationery to pin the corners down: eight, interlocking

1:25,000 scale ordnance maps, ordered from the Istituto Geografico Militare Italiano (IGMI) in Florence, Italian map-nerd central.

They were beautiful things, parchments, printed on heavy cream paper, artefacts of a pre-Google world: tangles of squirming lines and dots, trapped under an orderly black grid. Three colours were used: black for infrastructure (railways, buildings, roads and mule paths, forests, farms, chapels and 'notable monuments'); brown for the land (contours, gullies and ravines); and blue for water (rivers, creeks, dams and wells). The script was an elegant copperplate, the size of the font varying according to the place's importance. They were not, however, the most up-to-date maps. The keys in the lower left corner of each map told me that the first three maps had originally been surveyed in 1884, at a time when the cartographers still walked the land with theodolites in hand. The remaining five had been aerial surveyed in 1933 or 1934, I imagined by leather-helmeted cartographers flying low in biplanes. The key also stated that they had all been revised in the late 1960s, which was something, I supposed. I wasn't too fussed, though. It was a start. I loved them.

I hunted through the maps for the places that Carl had mentioned, and I circled them in chronological order. I then took out a pencil, sharpened it and carefully linked the places with a thick, grey line. It was surprising how, once I knew where I was going, the roads and trails that followed the logic of Carl's notes emerged out of the tangle of lines that covered the maps. I moved the pencil carefully across the contours, following the soldiers' progress. Once I'd finished, and the men had safely arrived at the Passo di Monte Moro, I opened the account that Cate had written and scanned through each section, studying the relevant part on the map. If I tried hard enough, I could see the men moving cautiously along the roads, meandering across the icy plateaus, celebrating in Alagna, zigzagging up to the Passo del Turlo, picking their way at night through the Nazi-occupied villages in the Anzasca Valley, and finally breaking from the cover of the forests above Alpe Meccia for the final scramble up to the Passo di Monte Moro and freedom.

I rolled up the maps, put a thick rubber band around them, stood them beside the desk and went back downstairs. The kids were doing their homework, and Carolyn was watching a cooking show on TV, dog on her lap, a rare moment of relaxation. I sat down beside her.

'Hey, Carolina,' I said with a rising intonation. She smelt a rat immediately.

'Yes,' she said cautiously, not taking her eyes off the screen.

'You know how I'm going back to Italy in September?' I said.

She nodded.

'Well, I'm really fascinated by this Carrigan thing. You know, the walk.'

She continued to watch the TV, adding nothing, leaving me to fill in the gap.

'Well, I've had a look at those maps, and I think the hike would actually be quite doable. I think it would take about a week …'

'So, you'd like to do it in September?' she asked. I nodded. 'Hardly a surprise, you know,' she added. 'As soon as those maps arrived, it was pretty obvious to me, if not to you. Of course you can. I don't mind. We'll be fine.' She looked down and patted the dog. 'Won't we, Beany Boy?'

I was overseas for extended periods twice a year and family life ran like a well-oiled machine in my absence, so they probably wouldn't even notice an extra week. I went back upstairs, opened my diary and started considering dates.

'Are you sure this is a good idea?' my friend Greg asked as we sat opposite each other in the ground-floor bar at the Trinity. 'I mean, it's a bloody long way …'

It was, in fact, around 100 kilometres. I knew that because I had used a map measurer, a handheld gadget with a tiny wheel that you ran along the trails on the maps, converting the paper hike into kilometres on the gadget's dial.

'And where are you sleeping anyway? You can't just doss down under a rock somewhere.'

'I don't know. I haven't got that far yet.' I shrugged. 'But I'm sure there are places along the way.'

'Maybe,' he replied, sipping his beer. He's a bit of a know-it-all. 'You are probably right,' he eventually conceded, 'but I'd suggest you get some better maps. I don't think those ones are going to work too well, especially in the rain. You can't really fold them up and shove them in your pocket, can you?' He patted me on the shoulder. 'Sorry. Just kidding. I don't mean to be negative. It's your life and, look, to be honest, I'm probably just a bit jealous. I kind of wish I could go with you. But I'm just saying, be careful. Plan properly. You're no spring chicken, you know. I mean fifty-eight, married with teenaged children ...'

'Yeah, yeah. I know,' I replied. 'I really do. Lots of people have said do not, repeat, do not walk alone. That's bushwalking rule number one, they remind me. I suppose I could join a group, or I could hire a guide, but where's the fun in that? I don't know. Being alone, walking into the unknown. It gives the whole venture an edge. A bit of spice. Maybe that is the point of it. I feel like I'm kicking away the training wheels, you know? Out on the high wire without the guy ropes. One last roll of the dice.'

'OK, OK. Settle down,' Greg said. 'Don't get too carried away. You're not crossing Antarctica. Yeah, but like I said, though, I wish I could join you.'

Eight months later I was on a flight to Milan.

The final walk from Macugnaga to the Monte Moro Pass.

Above: The main concourse of Milano Centrale.

Below: Biella, the start of the hike.

CHAPTER 2

Milano to Biella

Naked warriors and winged horses glared down at me as I dragged my bag rattling across the chequered paving stones of Piazza Duca d'Aosta towards the towering entrance of Milano Centrale railway station. I felt like I was entering an Assyrian temple. The marble and travertine entrance is over 200 metres long and 70 metres high, a mix of Arte Nouveau, Art Deco and High Fascist, as startling as the city's pinnacled cathedral.

The glowing white form of the station was a favourite target for Allied night bombers during World War II but fortunately it escaped serious damage. I passed a row of combat vehicles with joking soldiers and a pair of Aztec fountains before entering the cavernous 'carriage gallery', swept up by a stream of frazzled commuters elbowing their way towards the escalators.

At the top of the stairs, I weaved through a maze of suitcases, bored travellers, naughty children and panhandlers, heading for the counter of the Bistro Centrale. It was late August and a stinking hot day. Provisioned with a large panino, a bottle of water and a bag of lollies, I dodged across the concourse to the gates. Happily, my train was already in place, waiting at platform 8, a modest convoy of graffitied carriages sitting between two shiny, snub-nosed bullet trains, one heading to Rome, the other to Venice. Mine was the milk run, a slow haul west across the Po Valley plains to Santhià. From there, I would catch an even smaller train to Biella at the foot of the Alps to start my hike.

Apart from being a big white beacon for moonlit bombing raids in 1944, Milano Centrale played another important role in the Allied war efforts. A report produced in 1948 for the Italian government stated that the Italian resistance had helped 965 Allied service people escape via Milano Centrale railway station between November 1943 and April 1945. To illustrate their modus operandi, the report included an account of how six British former POWs were helped to get to safety in Switzerland. It reads like something out of a John le Carré novel.

The departure took place in Padova on the morning of 6 February 1944. A group of six British prisoners were accompanied by three guides, one of whom had been sent from Milan with the up-to-date plans. The prisoners were each given an overcoat, a hat, a pair of shoes and a scarf. Each one was also given some food for the trip, a false identity card made out with an Italian name, an Italian newspaper to read on the trip (or pretend to read) and a railway ticket to Milan.

An 'all-stations' train was chosen as this would give the prisoners more flexibility. The group was broken up into three pairs so as not to attract attention. They boarded a crowded central coach with one of the guides. The second guide went to the head of the train and the third went to the rear of the train. Checks by the Fascist military were inevitable on these long trips. Knowing that the checks always started from one end of the train or the other, this arrangement enabled the guides at either end to alert the prisoners in the middle as the check approached. In so doing, there was a good chance that the prisoners would have time to get off at the next stop and reboard one of the carriages that had already been checked. Where this wasn't possible, they would have to show their false identity cards to the military and hope that they wouldn't be asked any questions.

In normal times, the trip would have taken three to four hours, but delays caused by air-raids and damage to the line meant that they didn't get into Milano Centrale until after dark. They had therefore arrived after the curfew and so were unable to leave the station. They prepared to spend the night there. One of the guides was from Milan and had planned for this eventuality. As it wasn't prudent to stay in the waiting room, which was brightly lit and regularly checked, the group boarded a train that was scheduled to depart in a couple of hours. Shortly before the departure, the group moved to another waiting train and then another, et cetera, until the end of the curfew. At this point, one of the guides made the planned call to a local agent who was operating within the Milan telephone exchange, and the group was able to leave the station and walk to a nearby safe house. In this apartment they met another group of escaping POWs. They were able to rest until their departure, which was planned for the late afternoon.

In the meantime, the local agent confirmed that the escape route to be used that day was operational. The plan was to aim for the Swiss border above the northern reaches of Lake Como, 100 kilometres north, going via Dervio, Cremia and the Cavargna Valley. Given that they were travelling on secondary lines, it was felt to be safer to give the POWs single tickets for each leg of the trip rather than one single ticket for the whole trip. The POWs were supplied with the tickets and then accompanied back to the train station. Once on board, they repeated the same precautions as they had on the train from Padova to Milan, although on the secondary lines these checks occurred less often and were less rigorous. The group arrived at Dervio station after a two-and-a-half-hour trip which went via Lecco. It was dark by the time they pulled in.

At the exit to the small station, one of the guides took a torch with a blue filter out of his pocket and flashed it several times. The local agent who had been waiting nearby replied with his own blue torch and approached them. The two men exchanged passwords. The group then followed the local agent down to the lake shore where a boat was waiting. Here, the guides from Milan gave the POWs their final instructions. The POWs boarded the boat and were taken across the lake to the little town of Cremia. The Milanese guides spent the night in Dervio and then caught the train back to Milan, taking with them some of the hats and overcoats that had been discarded by previous escapees and that would be reused in future escapes.

When the group reached the other side of the lake, they were handed over to the local Cremia guides. After a short rest, they started their mountain trek, heading for the Cavargna Valley on the Swiss border. The climb was very challenging, 10 kilometres over three mountains with an accumulated ascent of over 2000 metres. It was very slow as they were hiking at night, there was heavy snow on the high ridges and the men had inadequate gear and were in poor condition. The guides helped the weaker men. Fortunately, there were no incidents along the way and the group arrived at San Bartolomeo in the Cavargna Valley after eight hours of hiking. Here they took refuge in the home of one of the guides.

That night they continued their trek to the Swiss border, another four hours of hiking. Several hundred metres from the border, they farewelled their guides, returning the equipment they had been lent, coats and hats etc., as well as completed records of their transit. The POWs then walked down to the Swiss customs point and the guides returned to Cremia where they prepared for the next expedition, which would happen in a day or two.

Apart from local variations, such as the means of transport, the season and the unforeseeable, this, the report noted, was the method used by the Service for the transfer of escaping POWs into Switzerland.

Sadly, Milano Centrale had other, less edifying, uses during the war. *Binario* 21, or platform 21, is in the basement under the far end of the concourse from where I was standing. Its entrance is on a side street at the rear of the station. Out of sight, out of mind. For a long time this hidden platform was one of the city's dirty secrets, as it was from *binario* 21, on 30 January 1944, that the first of twenty-three trains left under the cover of darkness with 169 Jews on board, headed for Auschwitz. Only five returned.

Persecution of the Jews in Italy started officially on 17 December 1938, when Mussolini's government announced the introduction of what are now known as the Leggi Raziali, the Racial Laws. These were primarily aimed at excluding Italians of Jewish background from participation in civil society. Similar laws had already been implemented in Germany, Hungary, Romania and Poland. Previously, the Fascists had not embraced Nazi Germany's obsession with racial purity and the new laws were not universally popular. Several government ministers, including Italo Balbo, commander-in-chief of North African Italy, spoke out against them. The proclamation of the Racial Laws has since been seen, in part, as a way of creating an internal enemy to shore up support of the extremists in Mussolini's own party and, in part, a way of toeing the line, of Mussolini ingratiating himself with Adolf Hitler and Nazi Germany, with whom he signed a military alliance two months later.

Things got even worse for those whom the Racial Laws deemed the 'enemies of the Italian state' after the armistice of 8 September 1943 with the Nazi occupation of central and northern Italy. On 1 December 1943, the Minister of the Interior, Guido Buffarini Guidi, sent an encrypted telegram to the prefectures of all the Italian provinces under Nazi–

Fascist control, ordering 'with absolute priority' the sending of all Jews 'to provincial holding camps'. It also ordered 'the precautionary seizure of movable and immovable assets awaiting confiscation in the interest of the Italian Social Republic'. Two months later the first train pulled out of *binario* 21, well hidden from prying eyes.

Binario 21 is unique in that it is the only European site that was involved in the deportations that still remains intact. The platform's underground location allowed the army to carry out on-site transport and departures in the most discreet way possible.

On the way from San Vittore prison to Milano Centrale with the first load of people, the convoy carrying Liliana Segre, one of the survivors, passed down Corso Magenta, a fancy street in a wealthy neighbourhood, where she had lived all her young life. She later noted all the houses had their windows closed that morning, shutters down. The city was sleeping; it did not want to see what was unfolding.

The prisoners were met at the station by armed soldiers with dogs who forced them to climb into cattle wagons. A hydraulic system lifted the wagons to the platform on the ground level. Here they were coupled to the locomotive, ready for departure.

It is estimated that in total 8564 Jews (of a population of around 43,000) were deported from Italy between January 1943 and April 1945, including 776 children under fourteen years old. Only 1009, or 15 per cent, survived, including only twenty-five children.

But the killing did not stop there. The same organisation and the same structures activated for the capture and exter-mination of the Jews also served for the capture and transfer to Germany of nearly 24,000 Italian partisans and political deportees, approximately 22,000 men and 2000 women, of whom almost half, 10,021, died in the Nazi concentration and work camps, mostly in Dachau and Mauthausen.

After the end of World War II, *binario* 21 was virtually forgotten for the next four decades. It became a neglected, rundown part of the station precinct, a shelter for the homeless and ne'er-do-wells. Its rehabilitation started in 1995. Every year since then, a local Catholic organisation, Sant'Egidio, and members of the Jewish community of Milan have met here on 27 January, Holocaust Remembrance Day. On 27 January 2013, a memorial was inaugurated in the presence of Prime Minister Mario Monti and other institutional and religious dignitaries and guests.

Pushing through the crowded concourse, I made my way to platform 8. At the bottom of the stairs to my carriage, a pair of smokers sucked furiously on their cigarettes, anchoring themselves to the handrails so the train wouldn't pull out without them. I squeezed between them and climbed into the carriage. Greeting my fellow travellers with nods as I struggled down the aisle, I located my booked place beside the window. I heaved my bag and my backpack onto the overhead shelf and collapsed into the seat. I positioned my provisions on the empty place beside me and settled in for the ride. Announcements were made, doors were locked. With a shudder the train pulled away. As the overgrown rail lines and abandoned signal houses of Milano Centrale slipped by, I unfolded my maps and spread them out in front of me.

The train arrived at Vercelli station an hour after leaving Centrale. Workers struggled to get off the train as rowdy school students clambered to get on board, shouting at each other and flinging their multi-coloured backpacks onto the patched seats, salmon swimming against the tide. Two African refugees climbed up silently behind them, standing beside their oversized bags near the door. As the train pulled out, a bedlamite, shirt ballooning, scuttled across the platform and down the stairs. Once past the outskirts of the city, we were surrounded by a sea of green: rice fields partitioned by low levies lined with poplars. Blue mountains filled the horizon. A white hump rose into the clouds to the north: Monte Rosa, my destination. The southern half of the mountain lies in Italy, the northern half in Switzerland. Until the English and Germans began scaling its heights in the mid-1800s,

Monte Rosa didn't have a name. It was simply known as 'the mountain of glaciers', an impenetrable barrier.

The train shortly stopped at Santhia, a small junction at the foothills of the mountains. Anxious passengers lined up at the door as we approached, jabbing the red release button until the train came to a halt and the doors slapped open. We had three minutes to make the connection to Biella. They poured onto the platform, dragging their bags towards the stairs. I joined the race. We clattered along the poorly lit concourse past a puddle of urine and then lugged our bags up more stairs to platform 4. At the far end, a toy train waited impatiently for us. The driver, her dark hair pulled back in a ponytail, stood on the stairs of her cabin, smoking a cigarette and glancing at her watch. Scrambling up the stairs, we claimed our seats, smiling at each other, grateful for the air-conditioning. The doors snapped shut and twenty minutes later we arrived in Biella.

The Anzac soldiers who worked the rice fields of Vercelli weren't the only prisoners freed on 8 September 1943. The people held in Italian-controlled concentration camps throughout central and northern Italy were also released, meaning thousands of Allied POWs were liberated. The British War Office has estimated that there were seventy-two prison camps holding nearly 80,000 Allied prisoners of war dispersed throughout the country. A clause in the armistice compelled the Italians to release the prisoners, though they didn't need much encouragement. Thirty-five thousand POWs were able to avoid recapture, and over half of those were able to escape Italy, either heading south to join the advancing Allies or north, like Carl, heading for Switzerland. The rest, nearly 18,000, remained in Italy, given shelter by local people, reappearing, to everyone's surprise, at the end of hostilities.

The clandestine Comitato di Liberazione Nazionale, the CLN, an umbrella organisation of the main resistance group, was formed in Rome on 8 September 1943. One of their first tasks was to help get the Allied POWs to safety. On 9 September, the military wing of the organisation appointed Milanese businessman Giuseppe Bacciagaluppi to set up a network to assist the POWs' escape to neutral Switzerland.

Bacciagaluppi was an excellent choice. He was born in Milan in 1905 and was married to an English woman, Audrey Smith. He spoke English fluently. He was an engineer and was employed by FACE, the Italian subsidiary of the giant American Standard Electric Corporation, which had a factory in Milan producing telecommunications equipment. Bacciagaluppi was a committed anti-Fascist. He lived in a large home in Milan and had a holiday home in Calde, a village on the shores of Lake Maggiore near the

Swiss border. He had already helped Allied soldiers escape across the lake before he was approached by the national committee, but it wasn't until November that his network became fully operational. In the meantime, spontaneous networks sprang up, the work of courageous individuals.

One of these was Dr Ferdinando Ormea. On 12 September, he was visiting family in Desana near Vercelli when he met some of the recently freed POWs. He decided to do something to help them. Using his own money, he bought the POWs civilian clothes and then accompanied them by train to Domodossola, where he organised, and paid for, local guides to take the men down the Val Vigezzo to freedom in Switzerland. When he returned to Vercelli, he met John Peck, himself an escapee from Campo 106, where Carl was also held, and an extraordinary character.

John Desmond Peck was born in 1922 in Sydney and grew up in regional Victoria. He was the son of a Royal Navy officer. He enlisted in the AIF on 15 December 1939, claiming to be twenty-two years old when he was, in fact, just seventeen. While training in Palestine his real age was discovered and rather than sending him back to Australia, General Blamey allowed him to stay in Gaza as his batman. He was eventually transferred to the infantry and fought in North Africa before being shipped to Crete.

On landing at Suda Bay in April 1941 he was involved in hand-to-hand combat when he and others were surprised by a troop of German soldiers advancing from the aerodrome. His battalion, the 2/7th, remained on rearguard duty to protect the Allied retreat and so were not evacuated from Crete.

Peck was captured but quickly escaped from the prisoner-of-war camp in Galatas and managed to evade capture for another year. During this time, he and a New Zealander, Noel Dunn, trained bands of Cretan partisans in infantry weapons and tactics. He met Commander F. G. Pool, a British naval intelligence officer, who helped him coordinate the escape of many prisoners from the island by submarine. Suffering from malaria, Peck was to be evacuated but missed two Royal Navy undercover submarine rendezvous. He was eventually captured again by an Italian patrol in May 1942. As he had an RAF radio with him, he was considered a spy, and was taken to Italy via Rhodes for trial. He avoided the firing squad, escaped, but was recaptured and sent to Bari Campo PG 75 in Athens. From here, he was eventually taken to Udine and Campo 57 in nearby Grupignano, joining Carl Carrigan and 5000 other Anzac POWs from the North Africa campaign. In April 1943, like Carl and his mates, Peck volunteered to work in the rice fields and was trained to Vercelli and Campo 106. He was held in a *cascina* in San Germano Vercellesi. He escaped at the first opportunity on 13 June 1943 (his fourth escape by this point) and made his way towards the Swiss border. He stayed on the lam for two weeks but was turned in by a shepherd he had asked for food.

John Peck was in prison in Vercelli on 8 September 1943 when the armistice was declared. According to his own post-war report after he was released, Peck met a young woman in the street called Adele Maschetti, who put him in touch with a local businessman and two priests who were willing to help buy food and civilian clothing for the freed POWs to get to safety in the mountains. Peck set up a committee to assist the POWs. He divided his time between this and operating with the local partisans. In his report he listed some of his achievements during this time, which included blowing up rail and road bridges and tunnels, blowing up the parachute factory at Cremenaga, and attacking the armaments factory at Saronno.

In early November, Dr Ormea introduced Peck to the CLN in German-occupied Turin, where he met Giuseppe Bacciagaluppi, with whom he collaborated closely for the next few months. John Peck was just twenty-one years old at this point. After the war, Bacciagaluppi reported in an interview that he had found Peck extremely dangerous to work with because he was completely without fear and had absolute confidence in his own destiny.

The work they did together was very perilous. Peck was arrested by the Gestapo on 12 February in the house of one of his collaborators, Oreste Ferrari. He was taken to Gestapo headquarters in Luino and interrogated and tortured for three days. On his twenty-second birthday, 16 February, he was taken to Como where he was tried and sentenced to death. He was taken to San Vittore prison in Milan to await execution, scheduled for 15 May. The day before his execution, he was under guard outside the prison when there was an Allied air-raid on a factory nearby. As the guards ran to safety, Peck scarpered in the opposite direction: escape number five. By the day of his scheduled execution, Peck was in Intra and back in contact with his organisation. By June, he had crossed the border into Switzerland. He returned to Italy and continued working as a partisan liaison officer for the British army until he was returned to England in January 1945.

Carl Carrigan's decision to escape early in September 1943 meant that he and his friends were unable to profit from John Peck's network or from Bacciagaluppi's service. They were very much on their own. They did have some assistance at the beginning, getting away from the rice fields of Vercelli and through Biella on the tram, but after that they were left to negotiate the 100-kilometre hike across the Alps to Switzerland by themselves, strangers in a strange land.

~--~--~

I hauled my bag out of the air-conditioned Biella station and into the mid-summer heat. My hotel was 100 metres away, down Viale Roma, a tree-lined boulevard built in the 1930s.

There are three parts to Biella. Piano, where my accommodation was, is the main part of modern Biella. It includes the elegant downtown that grew up within the medieval walls as well as the new town, a grid of low-rise apartments and factories, all sprawling across the plains to the south.

Piazzo is the original settlement, perched on a ridge overlooking the plains. It is connected to Piano by a cable-car. It is a tranquil enclave of patrician houses that stretches along a long terrace.

The third part of the town is Riva, a strip of land that runs between Piano and the banks of the Cervo River. The river was the source of the town's prosperity from the Middle Ages onwards and industries grew up along the banks, utilising its fast-flowing waters. The fleeces of the flocks of sheep that grazed on the high summer pastures were washed here and the mills that converted the wool into valuable cloth were built here, the water driving the looms. The wool industry thrived well into the twentieth century, with fashion houses like Cerutti 1881 and Ermenegildo Zegna gaining international fame, but it all took a hammering at the turn of the millennium when trade barriers were dropped and cheap imports flooded the textile market. Riva is still crammed with wool mills, but most are abandoned today, many empty, although some are being repurposed into apartments and community centres.

My accommodation was a four-star business hotel targeting travelling salesmen, a declining market. I liked it though: no frills, no attitude and all the mod-cons.

I entered the darkened lobby, shutters closed against the summer sun, and dragged my bag across the polished wooden floor to the reception counter. Silence. No one to be seen. I waited politely for a couple of minutes before gently ringing the little bell that stood at the end of the counter. Tingaling. Tingaling. Still silence. I supposed it was a quiet time of day in a quiet time of the year. I heard a door slam out the back and a middle-aged man hurried out, sweeping a grey switch of hair behind his ear.

'*Buongiorno*,' he said. 'Apologies for the delay,' he added with little conviction. 'How can I help you?'

'*Buongiorno*,' I replied. 'No problems at all.' I slipped my open passport across the counter.

'Just one night?' he enquired. 'What a shame. What a shame. There is much to see in Biella.' He passed a brochure across the counter. 'Now, I'll have to make a copy of your passport. Is that OK?' I nodded. Standard practice.

'Good. Now, here's your key. Third floor, first on the right. Not much of a view but it is a very comfortable room.'

'Thank you. I'm sure it'll be fine,' I replied.

'You're welcome,' he added, watching me as I pulled my

bag towards the lift. 'If you need anything, just give me a call ... I'm always here.'

I had a shower, changed my clothes and took the long hot walk into the old town along Via Torino. It was August, high summer, and the shops and cafes of this soulless street were closed, everyone having gone to the seaside or into the mountains. At the end of Via Torino were the public gardens, a little oasis of plane trees and shade, the entrance to the old town. In front of this was a cute building that housed the tourist information office.

The woman behind the counter was surprised to see me. '*Buongiorno*,' she said. 'How can I be of service?'

'Just looking, thanks,' I replied, moving towards the amply supplied brochure rack: town maps, an adventure park, a contemporary art museum, guided tours of the Menebrea beer factory (now they are talking), wool tours (wool tours?). I walked back to the counter.

'Actually, do you have any hiking maps?' I asked.

'No, not really,' she replied. 'Where are you going?'

'Macugnaga.'

'*Mamamia!*' she exclaimed. 'That is a very long way!'

I briefly explained my plan. Sometimes, when you present your ideas, your dreams, your plans, people's eyes light up. They get it. Other times, when their eyes don't light up, there is no point in continuing. This was one of the latter occasions.

'That's very interesting,' she said flatly. 'We do have

another Australian connection though. A lot of Biellesi migrated to Australia in the 1950s and 1960s so we often get their children or grandchildren who want to come here and discover their roots. And, of course, there is the wool. Australian merino wool is very prized here, so we have that connection too. But I'm sorry, I've never heard about these prisoners of war.'

'Perhaps it could be a new tourist angle?' I suggested. She smiled politely but didn't seem to be so taken with the idea.

On the wall, there were sepia photos of a tram standing in front of the building that now houses the tourist office. The lady told me that this pretty *arte deco* structure had originally been built as a stop for the Biella tram that started in the countryside south-west of the town and finished in the mountains at the Sanctuary of Oropa. The tram ran from 1925 until it was decommissioned in 1958.

I thanked the lady and went outside to have a closer look.

In late September 1943, Carl and his three friends had hidden in the back of the Biella tram, which smuggled them from one side of the German-occupied city to the other. The tram, with them inside, would certainly have stopped here. I looked down the street and I felt my first contact with the Australian soldiers.

Carl's odyssey had started a few days earlier. After being released on 8 September, the former prisoners stayed in the area around Selve, unsure of their next move. As German patrols increased, it became too dangerous for everyone, soldiers and civilians alike, so the soldiers decided they had to leave. A convoy of over one hundred POWs was organised. It headed north guided by an ex-smuggler, who Carl remembered as Petro, along with an Italian ex-army officer.

Petro was, in fact, Pietro Camana, a local man who became one of the leaders of the local resistance. He was born in 1906 near Pavia and moved to Vercelli where he married in 1925. He passed from one job to another, from builders' labourer to anchovy salesman. He was an anarchist at heart and hated the Fascist regime, finishing up in jail several times before the start of the war. He was one of the first to join the partisans after 8 September 1943, taking the *nom de guerre* of Primula, the Italian name for the Scarlet Pimpernel. His wife and two children also joined the partisan band. In February 1945, Pietro was killed in a skirmish in Sala Biellese, a small town in the hills south of Biella.

The other guide had quite a different fate. A reckless young army officer, Lieutenant Sergio Santucci is credited with helping over 200 POWs and other refugees escape into Switzerland, but he remains a controversial figure. In January 1944 he was forced to escape Vercelli and took refuge in the mountains. Here he played a complicated game of espionage, moving between the Fascists, the partisans and perhaps even working with American covert agents. In November 1944, he was arrested by his fellow partisans, given a summary trial, and was executed as a spy, along with five others.

The large, ungainly convoy of escapees headed north from Selve, taking refuge in a village called Vermogno, placing the sympathetic villagers in a perilous predicament. The following day, a woman ran into the barn in which Carl, his brother Paul Carrigan, Ron Fitzgerald, Lloyd Ledingham and Ron MacIntosh, another friend from Moree, had found shelter, shouting that the Germans were coming. The soldiers had already scoped out an escape route. They scattered. In the confusion, they lost track of one of the group, Ron MacIntosh. The remaining four hid in the forest until the Germans left. Once it was safe, they crept back to the village to look for their friend. They were told that Ron had been captured and had been taken away, destined for a concentration camp in Germany. Strangely, this was probably all for the best. Ron came down with typhoid a few days later and was hospitalised before being sent to the camp. With this condition he would not have survived the trek to Switzerland. Fortunately, he did survive the concentration camp, and was reunited with his friends after the war.

On their return to the barn, the group had received a cold reception from the villagers. It was night and the villagers were terrified of reprisals from the Fascist units. One can only imagine the state of mind of the soldiers. They were confused, with sketchy information and no plans. Most of them didn't speak more than a handful of phrases in Italian and the Italians rarely spoke any English at all. The soldiers had bounties on their heads. They had no provisions, and they were weakened by two years of privation and hardships. Worst of all, they stuck out like sore thumbs. They looked very different from the locals. They were taller and slimmer. They had different complexions and hair. They even walked differently. Most of them were still dressed in prison clothes. And they were on their own.

Carl and his friends weren't going to get anywhere without the help of the local people. The help could be as simple as ignoring the POWs as they passed by or not dobbing them in later. It could be an act of kindness, such as giving them a handful of cigarettes, leaving out some food and clean clothes or letting them bunk down overnight in a barn or a haystack. And it could be much riskier, such as hiding the prisoners, giving them shelter in private homes or even acting as guides to take them across enemy territory. The help could be spontaneous, or it could be planned but, either way, it came at great risk. If exposed, the helpers would suffer terrible consequences for themselves, their families and their communities. This could have been imprisonment, destruction of their homes, deportation to prison camps and even summary execution.

As Carl and his friends wandered the dark streets of Vermogno, they were approached by a young woman in her twenties, the girlfriend of Sergio Santucci, the ex-officer who had been guiding the convoy. She hustled them into a bar. She didn't speak English and none of the soldiers spoke Italian, but she was able to explain that she was taking them to catch a tram. She led them out of town in the darkness, downhill and across a cornfield. When the men saw a light approaching, they panicked and scattered but she was able to round them up and convinced them to get on board the small tram which had pulled up at a stop nearby, its windows blacked out for security. The tram rattled across the plain, stopping occasionally to collect and deposit passengers, with the POWs sitting quietly in the enclosed carriage, heading towards the occupied town of Biella.

Until September 1943, the war had not touched Biella directly. The overthrow of Mussolini on 25 July had been greeted with joy in Biella. During that night, symbols of Fascism had been torn down, streets dedicated to Fascist heroes were renamed with hand-painted signs and a huge ceramic bust of Il Duce was thrown out of the second-floor window of the Town Hall. The following day, factories closed, and the streets were filled with people sympathetic to the new government, including the leaders of the local socialist and communist parties. The initial euphoria disappeared when Italy's new prime minister, General Pietro Badoglio, the 1st

Duke of Addis Abeba and long-time Fascist hack, declared that the war was to continue. The factories reopened and life returned to normality.

Badoglio's declaration was, of course, a furphy, a ruse to buy time. When he and his cronies fled in secret to Allied-occupied southern Italy a month or so later, he left the population in central and northern Italy leaderless, without orders and completely vulnerable to the fury of their former allies, the German Reich.

Suspecting that the Italians were about to betray them, the Germans had been bringing additional soldiers into Italy since the fall of Mussolini. At the beginning of September, the German army had over 200,000 soldiers spread throughout Italy. This included the Leibstandarte-SS-Adolf-Hitler (LSSAH, Hitler's personal bodyguard unit), which was based in Reggio Emilia in central Italy. It was a battle-hardened division that had been moved to Italy from the Eastern Front in August to shore up German defences. The LSSAH was known as the 'Blowtorch Battalion' for the destruction of two Soviet villages where the inhabitants had been either shot or burned alive as a reprisal for killing two SS soldiers. The division was led by Joachim Peiper, who had served as personal adjutant to Heinrich Himmler, the head of the SS from September 1939 to October 1941. Peiper was an abomination and was responsible for a long list of crimes. He was convicted a war criminal in 1947, but never jailed (but that is another story). Peiper was proud of his division's bloody reputation, saying that it preceded them as a wave of terror, one of their best weapons. He liked to say that even Genghis Khan would have been pleased to have them as his assistants.

Once the armistice had been declared, the Germans moved quickly to take control. The LSSAH moved north into Piedmont. At Voghera, it divided into two. The smaller group went west to Cuneo and the larger group crossed the Po and headed north to Vercelli and then on to Turin. Their first priorities were to guarantee the continuation of supplicant administrations in the larger towns and then to set up camps to hold prisoners, made up mostly of members of the leaderless Italian army.

The LSSAH arrived in Vercelli on 10 September, the day the Anzac POWs began to move out of their confinement on the nearby rice farms. By 14 September Vercelli was considered a disarmed city, although the countryside was yet to be secured. On that day, a delegation of Germans entered Biella under the leadership of Major Moser. He met the local leaders, including several members of the council, and the head of the Carabinieri, the military police. Moser gruffly stated that the Germans did not want to interfere with the daily running of the province, as long as order was maintained. It was not to be a direct occupation. In the following days, the Germans issued a number of decrees, including an order that all members of the Italian army – officers, under-officers and soldiers, whether active or not – were to present themselves, preferably in uniform, to the tribunal in Ghemme, a town 40 kilometres east, near Novara. Anyone ignoring this order would be executed.

Despite what was promised at the initial meeting in Biella, on the morning of 21 September German soldiers entered Biella in force and the city found itself under occupation. While the LSSAH was relatively restrained at this stage, elsewhere they were up to their old tricks. On 19 September at Boves, a small town near Cuneo, 200 kilometres south of Biella, two LSSAH soldiers had been kidnapped by partisans. The parish priest of Boves, Don Giuseppe Bernardi, and local industrialist Alessandro Vassallo, acted as negotiators between Peiper and the Italian partisans, successfully securing the release of the prisoners and the return of the body of a killed SS trooper. Peiper had committed to sparing the town if the German soldiers were freed, but as they left, the town was burnt to the ground and twenty-four non-combatants were killed, most shot in the head with pistols in the graveyard.

On the same day, several officers of the LSSAH held a meeting in a small hotel in Meina on the shores of Lake Maggiore, 70 kilometres north of Biella. During the meeting it was decided to kill over fifty Jewish men, women and children who had been caught trying to escape across the lake to Switzerland. Three days later, the victims were taken to a local forest where they were shot. To cover up the murders, the bodies were then placed in sacks filled with stones, rowed out in boats and sunk in the lake.

Such was the world that Carl and his friends found themselves in as their darkened tram rattled through Biella on the night of 25 September. As they moved slowly through the town, the POWs peeped out of the windows and saw German soldiers everywhere.

The tram looped around the city, running past the factories and apartment blocks that lined the banks of the Cervo River in Riva, before curving around to the north of Biella. At this point, the young woman who had accompanied them gave the signal to alight. Once off the tram, they followed her through unlit streets to a block of flats. She told them to wait while she dragged a garage door open and then waved them in, closing the door behind her. She signed silence and then led them up several flights of stairs to a landing. She tapped on a door. A middle-aged lady half opened the door, startled to see the crowd staring at her. Her daughter hugged and kissed her and then waved the men into the corridor, closing the door quietly behind them. The men politely nodded to the lady as the daughter led them down the corridor and seated them around a table, taking their coats, placing a large flagon of wine and glasses in front of them. She then brought out a large wedge of cheese, a salami and a loaf of crusty bread, placed them on the table and told the men to eat, eat! They didn't need any encouragement. An older man, her father, came in and shook their hands then stood back and watched them as they greedily consumed the food.

The soldiers could hear the mother and daughter arguing softly in the kitchen and then the banging of pots. All went quiet and they started to smell the aroma of onions frying in butter. The old man came over and invited two of the men to follow him upstairs, which they did out of politeness, reluctantly leaving the food and wine on the table. At the top of two flights of stairs they came to a small room with a large radio at the far end. The man walked proudly over and switched the radio on, twiddling with the knobs. A plummy English voice began to speak to them – the BBC news. The old man was very pleased with himself. The men listened politely for several minutes but then rubbed their stomachs, begged their leave and walked quickly back down the stairs, worried all the food would be finished before they got back. By the time they arrived, a large metal pot of steaming risotto was waiting for them in the middle of the table. They finished the dinner off with shots of grappa and lots of laughter.

The average person's willingness to take extraordinary risks to help escaping Allied soldiers was much more than a political gesture. Mussolini had ended up dragging Italy into a war that was not wanted and which the country was not prepared to prosecute. It had been a calamity. All eligible young Italian men had been drafted and sent to war, ill-equipped and poorly led. In July 1943, Italy itself became the theatre of one of the most protracted, bitterly fought phases of World War II as the Allied forces landed in Sicily and launched their push back into Europe. Most of the civilians didn't see the young Anzac POWs as enemies. They saw them as young men, far from home, who had been caught up in a ridiculous and pointless war. More than one account records that the men and women helped the POWs because they hoped that, like them, someone in a foreign country would be helping their sons and brothers in the same way.

Once the meal was over, the family threw cushions on the floor and brought out a pile of blankets and quilts. The soldiers thanked them profusely, arranged themselves on the floor and fell asleep. Their trek to Switzerland would begin early next morning.

With maps and a pile of brochures in hand, I stood outside the tourist office in the heat, weighing up my options: go and explore the town or head back to the hotel, pack my bags and get an early night. I decided on the latter; I could always have a look at the town as I passed through the following day. I dragged myself back down Via Torino, sticking to the shade on the west side. I stopped for a beer at the Bar Brasiliana, just down from the hotel.

Sitting at an outside table in an arcade built in the Fascist style, I enjoyed the breeze while I sipped a cold glass of local Menabrea beer, and flicked through the coffee-stained pink pages of the *Gazetta dello Sport*. Despite being the middle of summer, with the start of Serie A still a month away, there was plenty of football to fill the pages. Players were being bought and sold; Diego Maradona was interviewed on Napoli's chances for the next season; and Mario Balotelli, AC Milan's freakishly talented striker, was being warned by Verona's right-wing mayor not to provoke the racist elements in the stands when AC Milan took on the locals. There was more than enough to fuel arguments up and down the beaches and resorts of the country.

There had been a change of personnel at the hotel. An elegant lady greeted me with a smile, handing me my key without asking for the room number. I asked if I could leave my bag at the hotel for a week or so and re-told my story by way of explanation. Like the woman at the tourist office, this lady had never heard the story of the POWs but, unlike the woman in the tourist office, her eyes lit up at the telling; she was far more intrigued than the other.

'I've never heard of that,' she said thoughtfully. 'We were taught a lot about Mussolini and the partisans, but no one ever mentioned prisoners of war. Our grandparents lived through it but never wanted to talk about it. Why would they? They were hard, hard times. I think people just wanted to forget about it. Put it behind them. I think it is still a bit like that, to be honest. Young people don't seem to have interest in history. Just those damned screens! So you are going to walk to Macugnaga? Wow … that is a long, long way. *Complimenti*,' she said. 'Of course you can leave your bag here. Just bring it down tomorrow. We'll put it around the back. I'll make a note and let my colleagues know. And absolutely no charge.' She laughed. 'That was a very nice story. Thank you very much, *e buona fortuna*!'

Once I was in my room, it was time to pack. I was travelling with two bags: a kind of soft suitcase on rollers as well as a small backpack. I emptied both and spread the contents over the bed. I figured it would take me eight days, seven nights, to get to the Passo di Monte Moro on the Swiss border, more or less the same time it had taken the POWs. It was stinking hot down here on the plains, but I could be walking through snow in the mountains and there was always the chance of summer thunderstorms, so I had to be ready for everything.

I hunted through the pile on the bed and began to lay things out on the floor. I needed two sets of clothing, one set to wear and rinse and a clean set to put on the next day. I laid out two fast-drying synthetic polo shirts (I like the collars – you can pop them to keep the sun off your neck); two pairs of fast-drying synthetic, multi-coloured undies; two pairs of thick socks made out of a bamboo fibre, which I was assured was a fast-drying material; and two pairs of very fine merino inner socks that were meant to stop blisters. I then laid out a pair of heavy cotton shorts for the day and a pair of long, synthetic hiking trousers for evening wear and bad weather. In case the weather turned, I packed a merino thermal top, a fleece pullover, a hooded Gore-Tex all-weather raincoat and a crushable felt hat that I had bought in a tourist shop in Innsbruck.

Then came the equipment: a 2-litre CamelBak water bag that inserted into the outside of my pack; a waterproof outer cover for the backpack; a silk sleeping bag and a pair of earplugs for the mountain-lodge dormitories; a head torch; a microfibre towel; sunscreen; toiletries and a small first-aid kit, including jelly band-aids for treating blisters. Finally, of course, my leather hiking boots, not to pack but to wear. I loved them because they looked gnarly, the type of boots an old-school Alpine hiker might wear, but they were heavy, inflexible and had no padding, hence my preoccupation with blisters.

I looked at the pile and despaired, knowing I would still have to fit in my laptop and chargers, a camera and a book, a slim volume of intense poetry, *Ossi di Seppia* (Cuttlefish Bones) by Eugenio Montale – a worthy book, which I would probably never read. With force, I managed to squeeze it all into the 25-litre backpack. I tried it on. The weight was fine, but it bulged into my back and felt like I had packed a basketball, so I lay the pack on the floor and sat on it, flattening it into an acceptable shape. I took out a carabiner, hooked it on the side of the pack and attached Uncle John's laminated photo to it.

I unfolded my two hiking maps again and spread them out on the floor: map #9, Ivrea, Biella and the Bassa Valle d'Aosta; and map #10, Monte Rosa, Alagna and Macugnaga. I lined them up so that the trail ran in a continuous line from Biella to the Passo di Monte Moro. I ran my finger along the squiggly lines from Biella to Macugnaga.

I knew I should have been walking with at least one other person. The negatives of walking alone are numerous. I would be going through some very remote places without phone coverage and I had no satellite communications. The only person who would know where I was setting out from each day and when and where I should be arriving each evening was my wife, Carolyn, and she was on the other side of the world in Sydney.

I had an app that I used to track the walks each day. When I activated it, it sent an email with a link to her. As she sat down to dinner with our teenage children, Gracie and Peter, she would hear a ping and know that I was on the move. If she wished, she could click on the link and watch my progress, a blue dot moving across Google maps – another one of those technological miracles.

I folded up my maps and slipped them back into their

plastic sleeves. I shoved #10 deep into the bottom of my backpack and squeezed #9 into an outer pocket. I had a shower, put on some fresh clothes and went back down to the Bar Brasiliana for a pizza, probably my last for a while. I walked back to the hotel, climbed in bed, ignored Montale and switched out the light. Good night, Carl. Good night, Uncle John. Let the adventure begin.

I woke up with a start four hours later, jolted from a deep sleep, my heart racing. I stared at the ceiling. What the hell was I doing? Was I fit enough? Would I manage to find the way? Would the weather hold out? What was I thinking anyway?

I closed my eyes, rolled over and tried to go back to sleep, but there was no avoiding it, I'd have to get up. I switched on the tableside lamp and threw off my sheet. I rolled out of bed and took a small bottle of *aqua naturale* out of the fridge. I walked to the window and looked out over the roofs of Biella, sipping the water, breathing deeply, waiting for my heartbeat to regulate, for my concerns to dissipate.

Calm restored, I climbed back into bed and pulled the sheet up. Maybe I should read something. I picked up Montale and opened at a random poem: *Dove se ne vanno le ricciute donzelle* (Where do the Curly Damsels go). I was asleep before I made it through the first verse.

Above: The Sanctuary of Oropa with
Monte Tovo in the background.

Below: The Upper Basilica of the sanctuary
with Monte Camino in the background.

CHAPTER 3

Biella to Locanda Galleria Rosazza
23 kilometres, 1500-metre ascent, 7 hours

The next morning, 24 August, I had a slow, greedy breakfast in the hotel's elegant dining room. I made a couple of ham rolls for the track, which I smuggled up to my room while the barista had her back turned. I slung on my pack, did one more sweep of the room to make sure I had left nothing behind and wheeled my bag to the lift.

As the lift descended, I patted my pockets: passport, wallet, phone. The survival trio. I left my small suitcase with the pleasant morning receptionist, who shook my hand and wished me well. I clicked on my trail app, stowed my phone and walked out the door.

I headed down Viale Roma again, waving to the waitress

who was wiping down the tables at the Brasiliana, and turned right into Via Torino, walking up this tedious street one more time until I came to the park where the tourist office stood. I kept going straight ahead into the heart of the old town of Biella.

Via Italia is a paved pedestrian street that snakes through the centre of town, the high street of Biella. It was early and the street was still in the long shade of the morning sun. It was almost cool and the good burghers were getting themselves ready for the day: shop shutters rattled open; plastic tables and chairs were dragged into position; delivery vans were badly parked in the side-streets; office workers with briefcases scuttled across cobblestones, already late for work.

At the top of town, at the end of a long arcade, I passed a sunny piazza on the right, which was closed off at the far end by the neo-classical façade of the church of San Cassiano. I learned later that this picturesque square had been the scene of one of the saddest, and most remarkable, events in the town's history.

On 21 December 1943, a German patrol heading north out of Biella towards Tollegno in the direction I was walking was attacked by partisans. Three soldiers were killed. Two young partisans were captured and driven back to Biella for interrogation. That evening five innocent people were picked up off the street, thrown into prison and held as hostages. One had been on his way to buy milk for his daughter, another had been helping his mate bottle wine.

The following morning, the seven prisoners, two partisans and five hostages were marched to Piazza San Cassiano. Here, they were lined up against the wall of a hotel. They were to be executed in reprisal for the killing the day before. A horrified crowd was assembled to watch. A firing squad of twelve German soldiers armed with machine guns shot the victims. Once it was finished, the officer in charge took out his pistol and walked amongst the prone bodies, firing the 'coupe de grace': a bullet to the head of each of the victims to finish them off. One of the partisans, a young man called Alfredo Baraldo, was still alive and conscious. He was eighteen years old and had only been shot in the stomach. He lay perfectly still, watching through squinted eyes as the officer picked his way over the pile of bodies, methodically firing his pistol. The officer had fired five times and was approaching Alfredo when the man beside him spasmed. The officer turned and fired his sixth, and last, bullet into Alfredo's companion. Seeing Alfredo's face, which was heavily marked from the beatings he had taken the night before, the officer assumed that he was already dead. He turned and walked away, reassembling his men and marching them back down Via Italia to their base. Three soldiers were left behind to guard the bodies.

Later, as the families picked through the bodies to recover their loved ones, a lady noticed that Alfredo was still alive and gently covered his face with a scarf so the guards wouldn't see. Alfredo waited patiently for his chance. Although gravely wounded, he inched his way slowly to the edge of the piazza. He dragged himself up and made a break for the nearby Hotel Gallo Antico. As he staggered into the entrance, he was spotted and one of the soldiers ran after him across the piazza. Alfredo headed up the stairs of the hotel and threw himself into a toilet cubicle on the first floor, closing the door behind him. He listened as the soldier's boots banged up the stairs and then cautiously approached the cubicle. The soldier banged on the locked door.

'*Occupato!*' replied Alfredo.

Incredibly, the soldier bought it, apologised and moved on down the corridor. Once he had passed, Alfredo opened the door of the cubicle and pressed himself as hard as he could against the wall behind the door, holding his breath as the soldier passed again. This simple ruse was enough to fool the soldier once more, and to save Alfredo's life for the third time that day.

With the soldiers gone, Alfredo came out of hiding. The owner of the hotel helped him down the stairs and across the piazza, where Alfredo took refuge in the church. From here he was able to make his way to the railway station of nearby Chiavazza and then on to his home in Vercelli. He re-joined the partisans three months later. Alfredo's *nom de guerre* had been Ciccio, or Chubby, because he was so young; however, after his experience in Biella, he became known as Evaso, the Escapee.

After the war, Alfredo returned to work as a stoker in the Vercelli hospital. He lived a quiet life, without any recognition, marrying, having children and becoming a grandfather, until his incredible story was uncovered by a journalist in 1982. Alfredo became a local celebrity. He died of cancer in 1995. The 'Miracle of Riva' was the only positive to come out of this terrible day.

Shortly after Piazza San Cassiano, the old town stopped abruptly at an intersection with Via Marocchetti, a busy road that ringed the old town, following the line of the medieval walls that had been demolished by the invading French in 1556. The Po Plain seemed to stop at this very point. Across the street, the foothills of the Alps started abruptly, steep slopes rising up to the village of Cossila on my left; you could almost put your finger on the point where the flat stops and the rise begins. Via Italia continued straight ahead, following the Cervo River up the valley towards Tollegno.

It was a busy corner, traffic coming at me from four different directions. I stepped carefully off the footpath and headed uphill to where I had seen a gap in the buildings. From here I could look down over river flats to a wooded hill hidden behind the Colle San Girolamo. The Cervo River itself was invisible, concealed by rows of three- or four-storied brick buildings crammed cheek to jowl, their red sawtooth roofs rippling across the floodplain towards the green woods on the other side. It was an impressive sight but also a rather forlorn one. These factories had once been woollen mills, the pride and joy of the town and the source of Biella's wealth, but they were now silent. Most of the businesses had either closed down or moved production offshore in the last ten or fifteen years, the victims of tariff wars and global trade, bringing a virtual end to centuries of tradition.

<hr />

Here, among the wool mills and workers' housing in Riva, Carl and his friends slept the night after enjoying what had been the best meal they had had for three years and drinking a bit too much grappa.

The following morning, the young woman woke them up with coffee and brought a pile of civilian clothes, which they put on, making themselves less conspicuous but at the same time less safe. The Geneva Convention stated that soldiers not in uniform could be considered spies and summarily shot. Taking their military clothes with them, the men crept out of the apartment block, crossed Via Italia and followed the woman into the ever-steepening nearby hills climbing towards the Sanctuary of Oropa.

There were two ways to get up to Oropa from Biella. The most obvious one was a twisting road that ascended from Biella through the villages of Cosilla and Favaro, following the same route as the tram. The safer option for outlaws was a small pilgrim trail that climbed up through forest, following the Torrente Oropa, a tributary of the Cervo River, towards the sanctuary. This trail supposedly followed the footsteps of the sanctuary's founder, St Eubesius. I was sure that this was the route the POWs would have taken and it was the route that I took.

St Eusebius was the bishop of Vercelli. In 369 CE, like the POWs, he escaped persecution, which in his day was by the Romans, by taking refuge in the Oropa Valley, high in the mountains above Biella. The route he took followed an ancient trading path that crossed the mountains from the neighbouring Valle d'Aosta and led down to the Po River plain. Oropa was a glacial valley scattered with erratics, giant granite boulders that had been dumped randomly as the glacier had retreated 7000 years earlier. With these strange formations and its dramatic setting, the valley had been a sacred site well before St Eusebius arrived. The story goes that when St Eusebius fled Vercelli, he took with him the congregation's most sacred relic, a small timber sculpture portraying a black Madonna, which had been brought back from Jerusalem. They believed it had been carved by St Luke himself. The sculpture was placed in a niche created by two erratics near the head of the valley and it has remained there ever since.

In the Middle Ages, the Sanctuary of Oropa, which had grown up around the relic, became an important pilgrimage site, supercharged in the seventeenth century when the dukes of Savoy, based in Turin, took an interest. More than a million pilgrims still visit the site each year. Sitting in a natural amphitheatre, surrounded by towering mountains, with sweeping views down over the plains, Oropa was as natural a sanctuary for St Eusebius as it was for the young rebels who fled the arrival of the Germans 1500 years later. The POWs knew this, and they had also been told that it was a partisan stronghold with a cache of weapons and supplies. It was the logical place to go.

After crossing Via Marocchetti, and so leaving the confines of medieval Biella, I continued down Via Italia. At the first curve, I took a small road up to the left. At the top of the hill, a marked trail lined with rickety wooden railings peeled off to the right, with a sign announcing the Sentiero Oropa. I took the trail, walking into a shaded birch forest, enveloped by the damp smell of decaying leaves and fungi. The path was flat and well-made, perfect for runners and family outings. Thick moss thrived on the stones in the shadows, topped by fans of lime green ferns, bobbing in the light breeze. It was silent, no bird life, just the sound of gurgling water running down old stone gutters beside the trail on my left and leaves rustling above me. I finally felt that my journey to Switzerland had begun.

The path narrowed and climbed up to the left, continuing through the dense forest. Below, on my right, a deep ravine fell away, cut by the Torrente Oropa, which crashed over jumbled granite rocks far below on its way down to meet the Cervo River. The path became slippery. It passed a smaller trail on the right that wound down to the Gorgomoro, a popular swimming hole that I could see below me. It was a chain of glassy ponds that cascaded one into the other, the water so clear that I could count the flat stones that lay like scattered coins at the bottom.

Further up the track, I passed an overgrown stone footbridge that spanned the stream at a pinch between two low cliffs. On the other side of the bridge, an old tabernacle peered through the scrub at me. I crossed to check it out. Inside, barely visible, was a faded fresco of the 'Madonna in

Extremis', who kept a wary eye on passing travellers. Further up the stream, I passed the remains of an old water mill, a ruined forge and a broken tower, part of the hydraulic system that once drove the looms in the wool mills of Corsilla.

I stopped to adjust my backpack, tightening the straps so the flat of the laptop fitted more closely to the small of my back. It was warming up and I took a suck of water out of the tube that wrapped over my shoulder from the depths of my pack. The CamelBak is an ingenious device: a plastic bladder that slips into the outside of your backpack. The thin plastic tube runs over your shoulder from the mouth of the bladder, and there's a rubber valve at the end. When you gently bite this, it opens, allowing you to suck water from the bag. The valve is secured to the front strap by a magnet, so it doesn't wave around as you walk but is handy when you need it. Genius. The problem is the taste. The early versions were made from waterproof canvas, so it tasted like you were sucking on an inflatable mattress. The product has evolved but just to be safe, I had slipped in a slice of lemon and some cubes of ice. I was happy. The demons of doubt that had haunted me during the night had disappeared with the morning light. I was glad to be on my own, glad the adventure had begun.

An hour after I left Biella, the path rose to an asphalt road. A small red-and-white sign nailed to a pine tree on the other side directed me back into the forest. Another thirty minutes on, the path forked again and I followed the signs up a steep hill, the first serious climb of the day. At the top, the trail wrapped around a high pasture. I leant on a fence and took photos of the views back over Biella to the plains. The trail then cut up into an older, more established forest, the canopy higher and the floor a silent carpet of soft brown humus.

Below the trail on my right, hidden in the shadows, the ruins of a modest farmhouse slumped into a bed of mouldy leaves. The black granite blocks of the walls looked as if they had emerged from the damp earth. Most of the roof was open to the sky, the few decaying beams somehow supporting a layer of stone shingles. Below the ruins were the remains of another house and those of a third, higher up on my left, perfectly camouflaged in the flecked light. The slopes on either side rippled like old carpet, the remnants of the terraces that would have sustained the families that had lived here for centuries. I wondered what had become of them. I supposed they would have drifted off after the war, the young ones first, heading down the hills to find work in the cities, leaving the elderly behind to tend the forest and the gardens. I imagined there would have been families living here when the soldiers passed. I supposed they would have rounded up their children and sent them inside as the strange men walked by, although I'm sure they would have given them a smile and offered them something to drink or to eat.

I kept walking along the path as it undulated through the birch forest until I came out at the first houses of Favaro. I walked through an avenue of blue hydrangeas to a small brick lane. It had been over two hours since I had left Biella so I took a flight of stone stairs on the left to upper Favaro, looking for a coffee. The only cafe in town was at the top of the rise. A young woman with spiky hair and tattoos welcomed me from behind the bar. There was a low stage in the far corner and a flyer pinned to the noticeboard told me that metal bands played here every weekend. I settled for a cappuccino.

'Where are you headed?' she asked as she banged the portafilter on a wooden bar to release the old coffee grounds.

'Oropa today, and then on to Macugnaga.'

She nodded approvingly. 'It's a fantastic hike. Are you staying at Rivetti?'

I told her I was.

'Say hi to Sandro for me. He's a great guy.'

'What are the bands like?' I asked, nodding at the flyer on the wall.

'Pretty crap,' she replied, 'but it's fun. They play every Saturday. Everyone is here. The place goes off. You should come.'

I laughed and thanked her but told her I was probably a bit old for that. Still, I assured her that I would try to make it the next time I was in town.

I carried my coffee to a table outside. I hunted through my backpack and took out one of the ham sandwiches. So far, so good. The path had been easy to follow and it had been a beautiful walk, a slow steady climb through a variety of terrain. Best of all, there had been no Nazis chasing me.

I retraced my steps back to lower Favaro and took a road that curved around to the left, passing a row of communal dumpsters full of rotting garbage. Two hundred metres further on I followed a stepped path that led steeply up between apricot-coloured apartment blocks. Behind the buildings was a dry-stone wall and above this a manicured vegetable garden with several rows of the plumpest tomatoes I had ever seen. They were dangling just out of reach. I slipped off my backpack and looked for a good foothold on the wall. With both hands on the top of the wall, I was about to lever myself up to the garden when I noticed a stern old lady sitting immobile at a window at the rear of one of the apartment blocks, staring at me. Caught red-handed, I held up my hands by way of surrender and dropped back onto the path.

My shame took me back to primary school, when I was caught shoplifting. I'd had to stand in front of my father and take the toy soldiers I'd nicked from Grace Brothers in Bondi Junction out of my school blazer pocket and place them on the hall table. Nicking vegetables was no way to repay these people their past kindnesses. Who knows, that old lady could have been the young woman who guided Carl and his friends through Biella in September 1943.

I picked up my backpack, waved once more and shouted a lame '*Complimenti!*', congratulations on your beautiful garden. Without blinking, the lady's steely eyes followed me as I walked up the stairs, across the field behind the flats and into the forest. I wouldn't have been surprised if she'd had a gun on her lap.

It was another long climb through beautiful forest for another hour until the path led me out onto a pasture with a farmhouse and a large barn at the top.

~--~

Carl told Cate that after leaving the safety of the family home in Biella, the anonymous young woman led the POWs up into the mountains. It was a long, hard climb and the weakened and malnourished men had had to stop regularly to rest their aching legs. Just as it was getting dark, they came to a farmhouse where they met a large group of young rebels who were drinking plenty of wine and boasting about what they were planning to do to the Germans. They knew the young woman and they invited the POWs to join them for a feed and a drink. Even though it was only late September, winter had come early in 1943 and the night was freezing. One of the POWs gave the young woman his army greatcoat to keep her warm.

They went off to sleep in the loft of the barn, with cattle down below to keep them warm. They snuggled into the hay and surrendered to exhaustion. The next morning, they woke up to find that the Italian revellers and the young woman were gone. Also missing were the buttons off the greatcoat. Buttons were a rare commodity in war-torn Italy but the inconvenience of a flapping coat was a small price to pay for the extraordinary risks that the young woman and her family had taken to help the soldiers. One hopes she survived the war.

Left on their own, the soldiers regathered their wits and decided to press on to the Sanctuary of Oropa. They intended to join the partisans and stay in the mountains.

I crossed the pasture and re-entered the thick forest. The path steepened. It was late morning, hot, and I was beginning to feel the effort. The path became less clear and the terrain boggy. I lost track of the markers, if there were any, and became disoriented. I backtracked and tried to pick up the trail again but without any luck. The map was no use as it didn't have the detail, so I put my head down and pushed my way uphill through the scrub. Despite the scratches and a torn shirt, it turned out to be the winning strategy. After ten minutes of bush bashing, I came across the track again. There had been a landslip and part of the trail had been washed away. Sadly, I realised later that I had lost my uncrushable Tyrolean hat, my talisman. It had been stuffed in my back pocket and must have gotten snagged as I scrambled through the thorns.

The track finally emerged at another high pasture, another farmhouse, this one with a trough fed by a strong running spring. I took off the backpack and rinsed the scratches on my arms. I then followed a wider track that wound uphill past a shrine to the Madonna and then on to a small asphalt road. I turned left here and continued climbing up the steep hill.

Although it was only a short section, barely a kilometre, it was arduous. Walking on asphalt is boring. Unlike dirt roads and cobbled roads, asphalt roads have no history, no stories to tell. They are laid out quickly and cheaply, burying the past. Walking on asphalt is also physically detrimental. When you walk on a bush track or a stone path, no two steps are the same. Each time you put your foot down on the uneven surface, your gait changes, your body adjusts, shifting your weight to maintain your balance and stride. Every step on asphalt is the same, repetitious, relentless. Jarring and unforgiving, it is bad for joints and muscles, only good for blisters.

I took the signed turn-off to the right and walked across a field, passing two surly young men, both dressed in jeans and singlets, leading three tethered calves to market. No greetings. No nods.

I followed a track paved with wobbly river stones into more forest. I crossed a small wooden bridge over a chattering stream and then walked out of the forest into another pasture, marked on my map as Le Alpe di San Bartolomeo. On the far side of the pasture, near the edge of a gully, was a cluster of stone buildings. From where I was standing, it looked like an abandoned farmhouse, which it was, but it was also much more than this. This modest pile of old stones was the Eremo di San Bartolomeo, the Hermitage of St Bartholomew, probably the oldest building in the whole of the Oropa Valley.

The first mention of the Eremo was in a document dated in 1207, but archaeological finds show that the structure already existed in the seventh century. The Oropa Valley in the seventh century would have been a wild place, its steep slopes covered in thick, primordial forests, an ideal refuge for people wanting to escape the violence that convulsed the plains. By the Middle Ages, the friars survived by subsistence farming and periodically venturing down to the villages lower in the valley to beg alms. They also took in pilgrims who ventured up to the sanctuaries, and wayfarers who were on their way over the mountains to the Valle d'Aosta.

An overgrown stone track crossed the pasture to the hermitage. The structure didn't seem to have changed much over the centuries. It was in good shape, neat and tidy with new slate roofs. There were the remnants of a large sundial high on one of the walls.

It was only when I walked under the arches, stepping onto the uneven paving in the cool half-light, that I began to feel the building's ancient past. In the corner, chilled spring water gushed into a deep stone trough. It was a welcome respite from the oppressive heat. I sat on the edge of the trough and ate my second panino, enjoying the soothing sound of the splashing water.

The last climb to the sanctuary was the hardest but it was also the most beguiling section of the hike so far. It started with a scramble up rocks behind the hermitage then followed a path that entered the most beautiful birch forest I had seen. The ancient trees formed a high canopy, snuffing out the undergrowth. Large erratics were scattered across the forest floor like giant sculptures. There were no birds. A thick carpet of soft brown leaves muffled my steps. The only sound was the rapid flow of a stream. The trail finished at the bottom of a flight of 150 timber steps, signed as the Pilgrim's Stairway. It was a hot, slow climb in stifling stillness, my last labour before arriving at the sanctuary.

At the head of the Oropa Valley is a glacial cirque surrounded by mountains; the sanctuary sits in the middle of this. It reveals itself at the last moment as you climb up over the lip of the valley, an infinite expanse of green stone, a spectacular ensemble of monumental buildings, a mountain Versailles, Baroque overstatement at its purest. It was completely unexpected and completely out of place. It is dominated by a towering neo-classical dome at the head of the valley and the courtyards that unfold in front of this are as grand as any of the Savoy palaces that surround Turin.

I don't know if the POWs actually made it to the sanctuary. After their night of hijinks with the Italian soldiers in the barn, they had set out for Oropa, with its promise of arms, food and camaraderie with the partisans. However, on the way up they encountered a New Zealand soldier coming down the same trail. He told them that a group of partisans had 'blown up' the ammunition and stores when they had spotted German patrols approaching. Carl was told that the partisans had then disappeared into the mountains.

Except they weren't partisans, not yet. These young rebels were actually deserters, soldiers who had defied the German decrees issued in the preceding week in Biella to surrender to the Nazi authorities and who had gone into hiding. They had taken their guns and headed to the hills. It had been a good decision. In a matter of weeks, over 800,000 Italian soldiers throughout Italy, their colonies, the Balkans and the Russian front surrendered. Over 600,000 of these soldiers refused to collaborate with the Germans, to serve in Mussolini's reconstituted army, and were progressively transported to Germany to work under appalling conditions in the factories that kept the Third Reich war machine going. Over 40,000 of them didn't return after the end of the war.

Survival wasn't the only reason these young men took to the mountains. For some there may have been an element of adventure, but for most it was also an act of protest, of defiance, inspired by the desire to resist, not to give in to the panic, fear and humiliation that prevailed in the occupied towns. It was a generational phenomenon with over 60 per cent of the partisans in Piedmont being aged between eighteen and twenty-three, and some as young as fifteen.

The 'rebels' survived off the generosity of those around them. They lived in shelters and huts in the high-altitude pastures that the shepherds used in the summer. Most were locals who could rely on the support of their family and friends to protect and feed them, but there were also deserters from other parts of Italy who couldn't make it home. It was estimated that in early September 1943, when Carl and his friends passed through, there were only about thirty young fighters operating in the mountains around Oropa. It wasn't until late October and early November, with the arrival of battle-hardened and well-resourced operatives sent by the clandestine Comitato di Liberazione Nazionale (CLN), that this defiance was turned into the resistance and the rebels became partisans.

Where to pursue the war – in the mountains, or on the plains and in the cities where the enemy was concentrated – was an issue hotly debated by the CLN in the early days of the civil war. The mountain strategy prevailed. In some ways, the partisans were safer here, far from the dangers and intrigues of the city and the complications of family life. War in the mountains was exhilarating. It was open rebellion, clamorous, declared, unequivocal. The bands lived together, they spent time guarding, patrolling and fighting together. They sat around the campfires debating, discussing, planning for the liberated country's future. It was heroic, and it was from the mountains that Italy's resurrection eventually came.

Carl and his mates were devastated by the news that the Kiwi brought them. There and then, they abandoned their plans of joining the rebels and continuing the war. With nowhere else to go, they decided to push on to Switzerland. They must have been shattered. Given they had no food and no provisions, no language and no gear, it was a very brave, probably desperate, decision.

They were, at least, in friendly country. The sanctuary itself was neutral territory, respected by both sides. Despite threats of bombardment by the Nazis, it was left untouched throughout the war. The closest it came to destruction was in June the following year when it was occupied by the partisans, who intended to use it as a base to attack Biella, but they withdrew at the request of the bishop, maintaining its neutrality and preserving the sanctuary intact.

～～

I sat on a low wall, caught my breath and looked around me. I was not alone. It was a sunny Sunday in late August and the sanctuary was packed. I made my way uphill towards the gate, passing an old tram that had been converted into a small museum. It was closed but I peeped inside and imagined Carl and his mates hiding in the back.

Everything about the sanctuary was large. I walked through the cast-iron entrance gates, into the first quadrangle. It was 100 metres long, with three tiered colonnades on either side that held bars, restaurants and shops on the lower floors and accommodation on the upper floors. The sanctuary can sleep over a thousand pilgrims. People wandered around, enjoying the sunny weather, laughing, taking snaps, kicking footballs or sitting on stone benches eating picnics.

At the far end, a broad flight of stairs led up to the second quadrangle, which was equally large. In the centre of this was a gushing fountain on a hexagonal plinth. Ladles were suspended by chains above the pond to allow the pilgrims to sip on the holy waters. Behind this, on the right, stood a small Romanesque church, the Basilica Antica, which held the celebrated Black Madonna. I filled up my CamelBak with fresh water from the fountain and walked into the church. It was dark and quiet, with hardly a soul inside. The air was heavy with incense.

I walked down the central aisle to the altar. Above it, framed by marble columns and fresh flowers illuminated by candles, stood the statue of the Madonna. She was almost life-sized. Her face was peaceful, with the suggestion of a smile, more an icon than a portrait. She held a golden apple with a cross in her left hand and balanced a more animated golden-haired baby Jesus on her right arm.

She isn't St Luke's original, which has disappeared without a trace – although this is not widely noted. This Madonna was carved in the thirteenth century, possibly by a sculptor from the Valle d'Aosta. It had been created out of a single piece of arolla pine, a slow-growing, high-altitude tree also known as Swiss stone-pine because it is so hard. She and Jesus are both very black, the result of a combination of centuries of polishing and the natural ageing of the wood, plus an unfortunate early attempt at restoration. She is wrapped in a cobalt blue mantle. Her dress and veil are sparkling gold, and she wears a gold crown.

At the far end of this second quadrangle was another monumental flight of stairs. At the top of these stood one of the largest churches I had ever seen, the Upper Basilica. It was commissioned in the nineteenth century to accommodate the increasing number of pilgrims and can hold around 3000 people. For me, the best things about it were the views from the top of the stairs back over the quadrangles to the Po plains in the distance.

I still had at least an hour to go before I got to my digs for the evening, so I decided to have a bowl of pasta and a glass of wine in a small trattoria outside the walls of the sanctuary to give myself the strength for the last challenge.

There are two ways into the neighbouring Valle Cervo. The first option is easy. It goes around the mountain, following a path called the Tracciolino, the little trail, that links Oropa with another religious institution in the Valle Cervo, the Sanctuary of San Giovanni d'Adorno. The Tracciolino leaves Oropa through beautiful pine forests and then wraps around Monte Cucco before curving back into the Valle Cervo. There are no climbs, just lovely views over the plains. It is the path that I would have liked to have taken, but it is not the path that the POWs would have taken. Once out of the pines, it passes through cleared terraces scattered with farmhouses. They would have had no cover; the rag-tag group would have been visible from miles away.

The other route is the hard option. It climbs up and over the mountain behind the sanctuary, then down into the Valle Cervo. I was sure it was the option Carl and his friends would have taken and so, despite my weariness, it was the option that I took too. It was a slog up a slippery trail through pine forest. It should have taken me an hour but I missed a turn-off just near the top. Instead of going right, I went left, following a faint trail through forest. After ten minutes the forest stopped. High above me rose the very steep slopes of Monte Tovo, a wall of rubble that spilled down into the valley. Far below me I could see the rectangular form of the Sanctuary of Oropa stretching out towards the plains. I wasn't convinced I was on the right path, but seeing a number of red walking signs among the stones I pressed on through the scree. It was like walking in fresh snow. With each step, my boots sank deep into the debris, sending a wave of rocks clattering downhill. I was worried I was going to follow them.

After another ten minutes of slow progress, the red markers disappeared, and I realised that I had made a mistake. I turned around and retraced my steps, striding across rubble, annoyance making me much less cautious. By the time I got back to the turn-off and saw where I had made my mistake, I had lost nearly an hour. It was getting late and I was well over it. Rather than continuing the scramble up to the ridge, I cheated and cut across to the asphalt road for the last section.

Happily, this detour introduced me to the works of one of the more enigmatic characters of these valleys: Federico Rosazza Pistolet, an entrepreneur who was born into a wealthy family in the village of Rosazza in the Valle Cervo in 1813 and died there in 1899. He had a colourful, carefree life until the premature death of both his daughter and his wife pushed him away from politics and business and into occultism and spiritualism, movements that were popular throughout Europe in the latter part of the nineteenth century. The tragedies also pushed him towards altruism, and he spent the last thirty years of his life building public works to the benefit of the people of the Valle Cervo. His collaborator in many of these projects was Giuseppe Maffei, an artist and architect, who also shared Federico's passion for the occult. They built many things throughout the valley, but their greatest work was the road on which I had landed, the *strada panoramica*, that connects the Sanctuary of Oropa and the Sanctuary of San Giovanni d'Adorno.

Like many great works, the road was a folly. Federico ignored advice from engineers and industrialists that a low road skirting around the base of the mountain was the best solution and instead followed Maffei's occult intuitions and went for a high road with a tunnel. The result was a marvellous piece of engineering, a narrow road that twists and turns up from the Valle Cervo to arrive at a narrow tunnel that was bored under Monte Colma. On the other side, it twists and turns its way down to Oropa. It is listed as one of the most dangerous roads of Europe and is loved by motorbike enthusiasts. Apart from the bikies and the occasional religious procession, few people now use the road, most preferring the safer and faster lower road, which was eventually built after World War II.

The most marvellous feature of Pistolet's road is the tunnel itself. It is narrow and dark and very creepy. It was cut by hand out of solid granite by stonemasons who worked in Pistolet's own quarries further up the valley. It took four years to complete the 200-metre tunnel. Maffei designed the entrances to resemble the gates to a medieval castle. After one hundred years of neglect, they were crumbling and overgrown with weeds but that, of course, only added to their mystique. The tunnel was barely a car-width wide and had no illumination. The walls were undressed, rough-hewn like an Etruscan cave. The only sound was the dripping of water that leaked through the roof, pooling around the paving stones. It was a deliciously spooky walk in the cool darkness. My only real fear, though, was that a squad of bikers might ride through while I was in there, which fortunately didn't happen.

It must have been the effect of the tunnel, or it could have been my tiredness, or both, but when I emerged at the other end of the tunnel, dazzled by the bright light, I felt as if I had walked into Shangri-La rather than the Valle Cervo. I was greeted by a breathtaking view across the deep valley. The most pleasing sight, however, was the hand-painted sign pointing down the hill to the Locanda Galleria Rosazza, which peeped around the corner less than 100 metres away.

The Locanda was another one of Maffei's Gothic

fantasies, built to provide accommodation and food for the weary pilgrims who had climbed the twisting road up from the Valle Cervo, either on foot or by carriage. Tacked onto the side of the mountain, the Locanda was a haunted house, complete with hanging arches, lookout towers and crenellated parapets. The winning touch for me at that moment, though, was the wide terrace with tables and chairs across the road, looking out into the Valle Cervo.

I walked into the bar, booked my bed for the night and then ordered a large cold beer. The young woman behind the bar sent me across the road to the terrace, and five minutes later arrived carrying a longneck of Menabrea beer, Biella's finest, in one hand and a basket of sliced bread and grissini and a wooden platter with slices of salami and prosciutto crudo in the other. I couldn't have asked for more.

Once I had finished my beer and snacks, I retrieved my pack and followed the waitress through a maze of stairways and corridors to a small dormitory that had three double bunks.

'Pick any bed,' she said, 'there is no one else staying. The bathroom is down the hall and dinner is served at 7.30.'

'*Perfetto*,' I replied.

Feeling pretty good after a shower and dressed in fresh clothes, I found my way back down to the bar and ordered another bottle of Menabrea from a large man with unruly hair and a friendly face hidden behind a patchy beard.

'*Australiano!*' he declared and looked me up and down. 'There must be a story.' I started to spin my yarn but he held up his hand.

'No, no. Not now. Tell me before dinner.'

I walked outside to the terrace, scribbled some notes in my diary, read my book and waited for dinner, watching the sunset over the Valle Cervo.

The dining area was a small room with a low ceiling. There was a bar down the far end under shelves groaning with bottles: red wine at the top, spirits and liqueurs below. Beside this was the door into the kitchen. With the sun gone, it was quite crisp outside, so a fire had been lit in the corner. Alessandro, the bearded licensee, and his wife, Maria, ran the kitchen. Gaia, the young woman who had served me the beer, and Claudio, a tall bald guy, worked the front of house. They were both students who had come up here for the summer.

There were no other customers, so Alessandro and Maria came out of the kitchen, dragged up chairs and waited for my story. Claudio and Gaia joined us as well. I felt like a teacher with an attentive class.

'*Dunque,*' I said, looking from one to the other. 'It was a dark and stormy night ...'

'Eh, no!' Alessandro reproached me, holding up his hand, waving one finger back and forward like a metronome. 'Tell the story properly, *per favore* ... I'm sure it is very interesting.'

I began the story again, but with a different twist. '*Sono qui sulle orme del mio zio John*,' I told them. 'I am here following in the footsteps of my Uncle John.'

They leant forward. I could feel their curiosity, their embrace. It was personal. I told them about my father and uncle growing up on a 'ranch' in outback Australia and how they had both signed up to go and fight overseas. Like the lady at the hotel, they all knew about the war and the partisans but none of them had heard about the escaping POWs, nor that the Australians had been involved in the fighting in North Africa.

Alessandro shook his head and laughed. 'Isn't that incredible? Our relatives, no, our fathers maybe –' he pointed at himself and then me, the two oldest in the room – 'were enemies. They were trying to kill each other. How absurd! How pointless and stupid!' He topped up my glass with red wine.

When I told them that John had been taken prisoner in El-Alamein, it was Claudio's turn to chip in. His grandfather, too, had been taken prisoner in El-Alamein but, of course, by the British. He had spent two years in a prison camp in North Africa.

'You won't believe this,' Gaia interrupted thoughtfully.

'My grandfather was also taken prisoner in North Africa like your uncle. But he was very fortunate. He was sent by ship to America and spent the rest of the war working on a prison farm in Idaho. He was treated very well. He was given three meals a day. I think he was even paid something. Not much, just pocket money, but he came home with some savings. He was very lucky. A long way from the trouble and misery at home. He never went back to America, but he always talked about it. America here, America there. *Mamamia, che palle!*'

In my new version of the story, John survived the Mediterranean crossing. He spent time in Grupignano and then ended up working in the rice fields. In my imagination, John had joined Carl and his friends. Carl's story became John's story. I told them about the confusion after the armistice and the thwarted plan to join the partisans and, finally, I told them about the escape route. They were familiar with the trails, and they were as impressed as the other people I had told that a man of my age should be walking on his own.

The Locanda was on the route of the Grande Traversata delle Alpi, the Great Traverse of the Alps. I told them of my plan to walk up the Valle Cervo tomorrow and sleep at Piedicavallo. It would be an easy walk, a kind of rest day. I'd then be fresh for the big climb up to Rifugio Rivetti the following day.

Although Alessandro had never walked it, it turned out

he was something of an expert. 'No, no.' He shook his head. 'That's a waste of time. It's only a couple of hours to Piedicavallo. Gentle walking down through forest. And then you'll have the rest of the day to get up to Rivetti. Too easy.'

The others agreed, nodding their heads enthusiastically, although none of them had done the walk either.

Out of politeness, and an innate willingness to please other people, I agreed and changed my plans. The meeting broke up and, as everyone left for the kitchen, Maria shook my hand. '*Bella storia*,' she said. '*Molto bella ...*'

I sat back and sipped my glass of wine. I felt pleased how it had gone with an engrossed audience. Italians are suckers for a family tale and I felt glad that Uncle John, and to a degree my father, had now become central to my adventure. I wouldn't be walking alone anymore.

I had thought I'd be having dinner by myself but, as the evening progressed, the door kept banging open and the dining room filled up. First a couple of ladies arrived, then a couple of young men and finally two families, including four well-groomed children. Unlike many places, the more remote you go in Italy, the better the food seems to get – *piu genuino*, as the locals say. Italians will travel a long way for a good feed and that was what had happened that night. It was a convivial crowd and there was an air of happy expectation.

Although polenta prevailed on the menu, Alessandro and Maria didn't define their cooking as solely 'Biellese' cuisine.

They had both originally come from Sicily, so amongst the more predictable mountain fare, I found southern offerings such as *caponata della Galleria*, Sciacca anchovies with Biellese butter, and *pasta alla Norma*.

As it was my first night in the mountains, I decided to go traditional and ordered the *polenta concia*, the classic dish of these parts. It was a soupy version of polenta made from coarsely ground corn, into which *toma*, a soft style of cows' milk cheese, had been stirred. It was once a one-pot meal for working families, a staple for battlers, but these days it's served as an entrée. I followed it with a generous portion of veal stew with roast potatoes and finished with another local classic, *bunet*, a very rich chocolate cake, unaware that this would be my dessert for the next four nights.

Dinner done, I thanked Gaia and the team and farewelled my fellow diners. I stumbled into the darkness, struggling to find my way through the labyrinth of dark corridors to my dormitory, and then regretted my decision to sleep on the upper level of the rickety bunk.

Above: Arriving at the Rifugio Rivetti.

Below: The path to Le Piane from Piedicavallo.

CHAPTER 4

Locanda Galleria Rosazza to Rifugio Rivetti
17 kilometres, 1500-metre ascent, 7 hours

I woke early the next morning and retrieved my clean clothes from the line outside the window. I repacked the backpack, pegging my still-damp socks to the outside so they would be dried by the morning sun as I walked. For better or worse, I had decided to stick with Alessandro's advice and combine the gentle Day 2 with the daunting Day 3: a stroll in the forest followed by a long and steep climb up to an isolated mountain lodge.

The whole team was already awake and cleaning up after the evening's meal. I had a croissant and coffee for breakfast and tucked a couple of pieces of fruit in my pack for the trail. Claudio said he'd do some research on the POW story and send me anything that he discovered. I thanked them once again for their hospitality. By the time I had finished breakfast, the sun had gone and clouds had crept in, filling the valley like an incoming tide. We all shook hands and I headed off down into the mist.

The Valle Cervo has been border country for centuries: a link between Italy on the plains and France which, until Napoleon's defeat in 1814, started over the mountains at the far end of the valley. Connected to the towns and cities of the plains, the lower Valle Cervo has always been prosperous. The upper valley, where I was going, less so. Life here has always been a struggle. Squeezed between steep slopes and a turbulent river, la Bürsch, as this end of the valley is known to the locals, is dark, closed and damp. There is little agriculture. What arable land is available, mostly hard-won terraces, has been divided into modest plots where families grow staples such as potatoes, beans, turnips and pumpkins. The few cattle kept here are taken up to the high pastures in summer and kept indoors in the cold months.

Before summer tourism, the only source of employment was in the sienite (a type of granite) quarries, most of which are closed now. In the summers in the old days, the valley would have been filled with the *ton, ton, ton* of the *scapellini* working the rock faces. In the winter most of the men would have left the upper valley to work as stone masons in the big cities.

By the time Carl and his friends passed through the valley, the quarries were still operational but had gone silent. Most of the men were at war or had taken to the mountains. The Valle Cervo had become a woman's world. Women organised the families and homes. They worked in the field, cut the timber in the forests and travelled down to the lower valley to work in the factories. After 8 September, many of them joined the partisan movement. A few became combatants but mostly they ran messages or carried materials and weapons up to their brothers and friends in their mountain hideaways. They were perfect for the tasks. What could have been more innocent than these young women pedalling along on their bikes; they were almost part of the landscape. The consequences if they were caught were, of course, as dramatic for them and their families as they were for the men who were caught.

A kilometre after I had left the Locanda, a curved white arrow painted on the road directed me through a gap in the guardrail, down two or three stone stairs and into a silent pine forest. I was glad to leave the road. As mentioned, there are few things worse for the feet or the joints than the pounding repetition of walking on asphalt. It is bad for the soul.

The POWs were keen to get off the roads as well. Their greatest fear was being spotted by roaming German patrols. Sticking to little-used mountain trails was tough but it was safer. However, it wasn't always possible. Carl told his daughter Cate of being forced to run 200 metres up a road to get to a gap in the forest. Carl was a hard man. He was fitter and faster than the others. When he heard a vehicle approaching them, he took off his belt, ran back and gave the laggers a couple of lashes to encourage them to safety.

The trail dropped steeply down through the pines, crossing the occasional switchbacks on the road. After an hour, I arrived at a group of houses. A rickety wooden sign pointed the way to the Tracciolino, the lower path that connected the Sanctuary of Oropa with the Sanctuary of San Giovanni d'Adorno. This path was another one of Federico Rosazza Pistolet's acts of beneficence, a footway for pilgrims to walk between the two holy sites. I turned left on it and headed towards San Giovanni. The trail was a little neglected, overgrown with grass and ferns, but that gave it its charm. It dipped and climbed through forest, crossing stone bridges over tumbling mountain streams.

My first view of the Sanctuary of San Giovanni d'Adorno was a bit disappointing after the grandeur of Oropa. San Giovanni is a single stone church attached to a horseshoe of cream buildings that curve around a large gravel courtyard with views over the valley.

Thirty minutes more of easy hiking and I was crunching over the sanctuary courtyard. In the centre an octagonal fountain stood on a stepped stone plinth, spilling fresh spring water into a large stone pond. The church was dedicated to John the Baptist. Its founding story is not dissimilar to Oropa's. Some shepherds found a wooden statue of the Baptist in a small cave in the side of the mountain. They tried several times to move the statue up to the higher pastures but it kept returning to the grotto overnight. A church was built around the grotto to house the miraculous statue.

San Giovanni is the heart of the *Bürsch*. It is the place where the people of the upper valley have gathered to celebrate, commiserate and to seek the protection of their saint for centuries. These hardy mountain people turn their noses up at the vulgarity and pretensions of the Sanctuary at Oropa.

The church was closed, so I settled for a coffee and a croissant in the cafe under the arches. Once I was done, I paid my bill and walked back onto the road. Above me, on my left, was a row of very old cypress pines, one of which had a large, faded sign nailed to its trunk announcing the Parco della Rimembranza. It went on to explain that the park of remembrance commemorates the people of the valley who had lost their lives in all wars. It was therefore a sacred place. Picnics and parking here were forbidden.

A gravel path wrapped around under the low walls of a small memorial garden. On either side of the path were neat rows of small sienite blocks. Each block had a bronze plaque attached to it with the name, rank, date of birth and date of death of the *valligiano* (the valley-dweller) who had died. There were some soldiers who had died in battles for Italian independence in the 1850s and others who had died in the First World War, but most of the markers commemorated people who had been killed in World War II. Most were very young and all were male: Partigiano Bergometti Giacinto: 7-10-1924 to 6-4-1945; Partigiano Perico Walter: 3-1-1920 to 21-11-1944; Corporale Lodino Pietro: 15-11-1906 to 4-10-1944. Partisans were commemorated beside Fascists. There was no distinction. This well-tended park was an articulate expression of the strength of identity of this small mountain community.

Seventy years later all was forgiven, but such an ecumenical spirit was not always the case. With the unionised industries in the lower valley and the steep, impenetrable slopes of the upper valley, the Valle Cervo was an anti-Fascist stronghold. Bands of deserting soldiers took to the high country with their weapons to avoid the Fascist round-ups and founded the first partisan groups in the valley, skirmishing with the enemy.

It was guerrilla warfare. They avoided head-on confrontations, instead attacking and then retreating back into the mountains. The rebels' deep knowledge of the area was a great advantage, and this was recognised by the Fascists. The bandits, as the Fascists called them, belonged to the valley. They knew all the paths, the huts and the ravines. They knew how many hours it would take the Fascist forces to reach a ridge and what route they would follow. They knew the obstacles and uncertainties that would delay the enemy. They had informants, runners who would carry messages up to their shelters, and they had secret alarm signals.

However, it was the support of the local population that was the partisans' greatest strength, and their enemy was aware of this too. Unable to win the locals' hearts and minds, the Germans and Fascists turned to terror in their attempt to break the nexus. In 2009 the Italian and the German governments established a joint commission to work on a critical analysis of their common experience during World War II. As a result, it was possible to paint a complete picture of the violence perpetrated against civilians by the German army and its Fascist allies in Italy between 1943 and 1945. The commission's findings were published in 2016 as the *Atlas of Nazi and Fascist Massacres in Italy* and are available online. More than 5000 episodes were counted and listed in the database, each one of them was retraced and set in its specific time and war frame and, when possible, the identity of the victims and the perpetrators was established. The commission estimated that more than 22,000 innocent Italian citizens were murdered in massacres and reprisal killings between 8 September 1943 and 25 April 1945. Only a handful of Nazi war criminals were ever prosecuted for these events, and even less served time in an Italian prison. Few German soldiers accused or convicted of taking part in these war crimes showed any remorse for their actions.

Partisan actions against Carabinieri Fascist centres in the valleys surrounding Biella were part of this pattern and were met with vicious reprisals: summary executions in a series of villages in the lower Valle Cervo, including Valle Mosso and Cossato. These killings, meant to intimidate and break the local support for the partisans, only hardened the people's resolve.

This is not to say that the partisans and the resistance were always the good guys. There are plenty of reports of partisan groups stealing food and victuals, of cattle and sheep rustling and of random killings. After 25 April 1945, Liberation Day, a score-settling campaign ensued against pro-German collaborators, known in Italian as *il resa dei conti*. Many were publicly humiliated, paraded naked in the streets or tarred and feathered, while many others were speedily court-martialled, condemned and shot, or just shot. Official estimates after the war were around 800 victims, but later research has come up with far greater numbers, variously estimated to be around 10,000 victims. Dark days, indeed.

Carl Carrigan and his mates weren't the only people retreating to the safety of the Valle Cervo, escaping the violence on the plains. Many families, women and children evacuated to the Valle Cervo from the big cities and towns as the Allied night bombings increased, bunking down with relatives or opening up their holiday homes. Jewish families took refuge here as well, finding a hideout in the Valle Cervo on their way to Switzerland.

The Jonas were one such family; they had lived in Piazzo, the old town of Biella, for over 400 years. The father was a well-known lawyer, and it was through this connection that five members of his family and their nanny were given refuge in October 1943 in the holiday house of a colleague in Bariola, a tiny hamlet a short walk downhill from the Sanctuary of San Giovanni. In December they were forced to move further up the valley to Valmosca, where an elderly seamstress gave them refuge until the end of the war, eighteen months later.

Elena Accati, who was a young girl living in the Valle Cervo during the war, wrote about the story of a less fortunate family. One day in the winter of 1943–44, her uncle came to visit and told them that he had recently found accommodation for a Jewish family, two adults and a small boy, in an abandoned farmhouse in the valley. He organised food for them and told them not to leave the house. Shortly after, there was a heavy snowfall. Thinking themselves safe, the family went outside for a short walk. Someone saw their footsteps in the snow and reported them to the authorities. They were taken away and never seen again.

I left the memorial gardens and continued on my way down into the valley. On the first curve, a sign pointed off to the right to a solidly built stone path, three metres wide, its flagstones covered in a layer of decaying leaves and moss. It led me downhill through a forest of beech, ash trees and oaks, their trunks wrapped in ivy, the rocks at the base covered in lichens, moss and ferns. I came to a small chapel, where the path forked.

One of Carl's friends, Lloyd Moule, also a prisoner in Vercelli, headed for Switzerland a month later, at the end of October. In his memoir, Lloyd writes that as his group was walking, they too came to a fork in the path. A young 'angelic' boy aged around ten came running up to them. The boy shouted, '*Tedeschi! Tedeschi!*' (Germans! Germans!) and implored them not to go down to the right as the Germans were in the village at the end of the path. Most of the group thought it was a trap and didn't want to listen. The boy became more distressed. Lloyd managed to convince the others to take the boy's advice. It was just as well they did, as Germans did go to the village identified by the child and proceeded to kill many people for assisting the partisans. Lloyd later said that he believed the boy had been an angel sent to save them. Lloyd and his friends took a different route from Carl, but I remembered the story, and I liked to think that this fork, with its ancient chapel, was also watched over by the forces of good.

I too chose the left fork and continued down through the forest, passing another chapel before coming to a footbridge that arched over a stream and took me into a small hamlet. A flight of stairs led me up to the asphalt road again and I followed this down to the Cervo River.

I crossed a bridge and arrived at the main road that ran the length of the valley. No footpaths, of course. I had to shimmy my way around a blind corner, avoiding a stream of trucks and cars cutting the bend. Once around, the river flat widened. I passed an ornamental footbridge on the right, which led to a small cemetery carved into a rock escarpment. I then passed tennis courts before arriving at Rosazza, the home of Federico Rosazza Pistolet.

Federico's kooky influence is evident as soon as you enter the village. In the 1880s he and his collaborator, Giuseppe Maffei, transformed this quiet mountain village into a neo-Gothic fantasy. His first project was to pull down the ancient stone parish church and relocate the cemetery to the other side of the river. This created enough space to build a very large Tuscan-inspired Romanesque church, which had nothing at all to do with the austere mountain architecture that surrounded it. Further up the hill, he built himself a mock-medieval castle, complete with a colonnade based on the ruins of Paestum; an Etruscan arch modelled on the entrance to Volterra; and a circular tower with Guelf battlements that stared gloomily down at the Torrente Paghetta. In the main square, the municipal offices were rebuilt as a striped Sienese palace, with a long arcade of spindly columns capped by carved capitals. The arcade is connected to an 80-metre-high belltower that is topped with Ghibelline battlements. Inside the belltower is a curling white marble staircase that leads up to a lookout with spectacular views over the valley. Equally impressive buildings surround the square.

All that has survived of the old village has been pushed up into the wings, where five-storey apartment blocks with small windows, iron balconies and stone roofs crowded together creep up the side of the mountain, shyly peeping over the terracotta roofs of the palazzi. There are not many permanent residents these days, a few oldsters hanging out in the bar, a mother with a pram doing her shopping in the little *alimentari*. Today Rosazza has a population of less than one hundred, well down from its peak in Federico's day of around 1500.

I continued uphill out of town, leaving the asphalt road to cross over the river along an old stone bridge. On the other side, I picked up a trail that wound up through forest, eventually widening out to green pastures known as *fianbello*, or 'the good hay'. On the other side was a fast-running stream, the Chiobba Torrente, a tributary that spilled into the Cervo River. There were a couple of old stone shelters on the upper side of the fields that had collapsed and were slowly being swallowed up by the forest. In the middle of one was the remains of a campsite, charred logs surrounded by empty bottles, used condoms and other debris of teenage romance.

I picked my way gingerly across the stream and then climbed a long flight of stairs into the pretty hamlet of Montesinaro, a cluster of stone houses that sat on top of a hill wedged between the two waterways. At the top of the stairs was a narrow lane that continued to climb up, squeezing between the tall houses. I stopped for a breather and complimented an elderly lady who was on her knees digging in a bed of exuberant flowers. She laughed and stood up, thanking me modestly. She wandered over for a chat. In response to her question, I told her my, by now, well-rehearsed story. She listened carefully, nodding her head as I progressed. When I had finished, she told me that there was a similar story associated with her village.

'After the armistice in September 1943, three Allied soldiers, they could have been Australians, had made their way up the valley to Montesinaro,' she said. 'They had been taken in by a family in the hamlet, the Bosazzas, and had spent the rest of the war hiding in their home. I don't know exactly where the house was.' She waved her hand uphill. 'Somewhere up the top.'

The story went that these soldiers, maybe three but there could have been more, were on their way to Switzerland when they met a local retired engineer, Giorgio Bosazza, who had learned good English when he worked in Africa before the war broke out. He was well-off, had a large home and gave them shelter.

One night not long after their arrival, there was banging outside and a patrol of German soldiers stood at the door, demanding to be fed. Ordinarily, Giorgio would have resisted or, at most, given the bare essentials, but this time, not wanting any trouble, he ushered them in without question. A pot of polenta was immediately prepared and dressed in the last of their butter, a luxury at the time. After an hour of terror, the sated Germans left.

Several days later, the POWs were moved from Montesinaro, taken further down the valley to Rialmosso, where they set up camp in an abandoned seventeenth-century sulphur mine, high up the side of a mountain. There they spent the rest of their time until 25 April 1945, when victory over the Fascists was declared. All that time, Giorgio or his wife regularly carried provisions to them – potatoes and whatever else they could spare – a two-hour walk along trails facing the usual dangers. Everyone in the village knew of the arrangements but no one talked, not even the young ones; they were all well aware of the reprisals and perils. In this period even the walls and the air had ears to listen and eyes to spy. In a recent interview, Maria, Giorgio's daughter, said she couldn't understand how her four-year-old self managed to keep this exciting secret but it was just as well she did because if they had been caught their house would have been burned, with them in it.

Giorgio kept a diary, which he left to Maria. In this, he described the POWs as brothers, worthy young men who deserved their help and affection. From the day victory was declared, he wrote, the prisoners were free British citizens, no longer men of the forest, hunted like wild animals by the Fascists and Nazis.

I took my leave from the *signora* and continued on to Piedicavallo, which was only a kilometre away, connected to Montesinaro by a back road that ran along a terrace, high above the river. Piedicavallo is at the head of the valley, a small village completely enclosed by soaring mountains. The lower slopes are covered in thick forests. The peaks were scarcely visible from the town, just a couple of glimpses, bare and jagged rocks that only hinted at the wilderness that lay beyond them.

There are two theories as to how this village got its strange name, which literally translates as 'horses' feet'. The first is that in the past, Piedicavallo was the last place in the valley that you could reach on horseback, travellers having to walk beyond this. The other, more plausible, theory is that the name is a corruption of the old dialect term *Pe' d'cò d'val*, meaning the foot of the mountains.

Piedicavallo may be the end of the road, but it isn't the end of the world, or wasn't in times gone by. For centuries the world came to Piedicavallo. Rather than being a barrier, the mountain range that soars up behind the village was its connection to a wider world. Two ravines converge on the town. If you walk straight on through Piedicavallo, a very steep winding path takes you up one of these ravines to the Porta della Vecchia pass at 2187 metres. For centuries this was the border between Italy and France, a gateway into the Valle d'Aosta. Archaeologists believe that people have been coming and going across this pass since at least the fourth century CE.

If you walk up to the right of Piedicavallo heading north, the second ravine climbs up to the Passo della Mologna Grande, 2493 metres. From here a convoluted series of trails leads across a barren high plateau to the German-speaking valleys that radiate around the slopes of Monte Rosa. A small but steady stream of game travellers used these trails for centuries. It was the same route that Carl and his friends took.

With its tall stone buildings, narrow lanes, geranium

boxes and a Baroque church, Piedicavallo is a classic Alpine village. Summer was over when I got there. The streets were empty, the window shutters closed, the doors locked. The only sign of life was at the bar in the village's only hotel, the Albergo Rosa Bianca. It was on the right as I entered the village, and it was open for lunch. The pleasant aroma that greeted me as I passed the open window was far more appealing than the two pieces of fruit I had in the outer pocket of my backpack so I decided to stop and grab a bite to eat. Besides, I was tired and hungry, and I would need the energy to confront the challenge that was ahead of me.

I was told by the lady behind the reception desk that the hotel had been in the same family since it opened in 1856. She showed me to a small table under the window. Ten minutes later a large bowl of steaming *tortellini boscaiola*, a cream and mushroom sauce, was placed in front of me. In my enthusiasm, I ordered a *quartino*, a small carafe, of white wine to wash it down.

By the time I had finished my meal and was back out on the street, the temperature had dropped, the clouds were even lower, and I started to think about rain. It was half past two. I had one of the most challenging sections of the hike in front of me, straight up the northern ravine to the Rifugio Rivetti, the mountain hut where I would be staying the night. It was situated on a bluff just below the Passo della Mologna Grande. It was only 6 kilometres away, but there was a 1500-metre climb to get there.

I walked up the narrow Via Roma, which was paved with river stones slick from the green slime that thrived in the permanent half-light. At the top of the hill, the street opened out into a small piazza dominated by the parish church. A wide flight of shallow stone stairs continued uphill to the right of the church, the beginning of my climb. There was a hiking map attached to the church wall. Beside this was a sign with a red and white arrow, pointing uphill: 'Rifugio Rivetti, 3 hours'.

The blue sky of the morning had been covered by low cloud. It was cool and the air was damp. Perfect weather for hiking, as long as it didn't rain. I was confident I could get there before dark but I got off to a slow start. I had to stop to catch my breath before I'd even left the village, the tortellini and wine sitting heavily in my stomach.

There are no mountains where I live, just parks and beaches. My fitness regime had involved jogging around the periphery of the local park two or three times a week, complemented by a reluctant program of light weight-bearing exercises at the neighbourhood gym. Not ideal for a long hike in the mountains, but not too bad. I put my head down and picked up the pace.

Once out of the village, I found my stride. It was exhilarating to be climbing up through lush forest following an ancient stone path under dripping trees. It was goblin country. The path had been untouched for decades and had almost become part of the mountain. A retaining wall on my right, made of crude blocks of roughly hewn granite, leant on the mountain, pushing against its implacable descent into the valley. The large granite paving stones were grouted with rotten leaves. They were cracked and broken by landslips but still held their positions. Twenty metres over the edge on my left, out of sight behind thick undergrowth, the Mologna Torrent raged through a jumble of boulders.

After twenty minutes, the path levelled and I emerged out of the forest to a collection of stone houses, Le Piane di Piedicavallo. One of the houses, down on my left near the stream, was open, washing flapping in the breeze, but the rest of them were bolted shut. In the not-so-distant past, once the snows had melted, the men of the valley would have brought their cattle up here to graze on the *siun*, the nutritious grass only found in the high summer pastures. The cattle would be milked each day, rounds of cheese made and stored in small stone outhouses, usually close to the stream to keep them cool and moist. Every now and then, the men would head back down the hill to take the cheese to market, carried on the back of a donkey. When the first snows returned, the houses would be closed up and the men and animals would go back down to the valley. The animals would be corralled for the winter but the men wouldn't stay home for long. Times were tough and they would leave the valley for work in the 'bad season', often finding employment as stonemasons in the big cities on the plains.

When Carl and his friends climbed out of the Valle Cervo, they came to a stone hut that had a stack of wood outside. This was probably Le Piane, as there were no other settlements and little forest above this. Although it was still September, winter came early in 1943 and it was already cold. The exhausted men went inside to make a fire. As they warmed themselves, the door burst open and five large woodcutters came in. Carl and his friends retreated to the far end of the hut. It was a small hut but the woodcutters managed to ignore the soldiers, not addressing a single word to them. The woodcutters stoked the fire and grilled a handful of small birds over the coals. The starving soldiers sat silently, watching them eat. With the meal finished, the woodcutters cleaned up the fire, put on their coats and left, without acknowledging the POWs nor leaving them any scraps. Once the woodcutters were well gone, the soldiers returned to the fire, made beds out of hay and leaves and lay down for their last warm sleep for several days.

Three days later, the men arrived at the village of Sant'Antonio, where the Valle Vogna meets the Valsesia. To get there, they had climbed three passes and followed unmarked trails across 40 kilometres of uninhabited glacial wasteland without adequate clothing and with no food. It's difficult to imagine the hardship they must have endured.

By the time I left Le Piane, the clouds had closed in, the temperature had dropped and a light drizzle had started. As I left the hamlet, following a small, paved path between low dry-stone walls, two donkeys farewelled me from a field of cut grass on the right. The path became a rough stone trail as I climbed, still following the course of the torrent. The vegetation changed as well. The lush birch forest with its moss and ferns gradually gave way to rocky fields covered with thick tufts of long grasses scattered with stands of spindly silver birch and scraggly pines. The drizzle had turned to rain and I took shelter under one of the dripping trees to get out my wet weather gear: a Gore-Tex raincoat and a plastic cover for the backpack.

The path began to zigzag, tacking up away from the trees and the gully. I could see little ahead of me but steep slopes of scree, boulders and low cloud. Although it was the end of August, I had expected to pass other hikers but I had seen no one since leaving Piedicavallo. I was still travelling quite well though. I had found my stride, that sweet spot between the initial pain and the final exhaustion. I stopped at every second bend to catch my breath, leaning forward to give my shoulders a break from the weight on my back. The rain became heavier and I slipped twice, having lost my balance because of the offset pack, and slowly tumbled onto the wet grass, muddying my hands and knees but doing myself no injuries. The rain kept falling.

An hour after I'd left Le Piane, the path levelled out again, opening onto a wide meadow strewn with granite boulders, the Alpe Anval Superiore. On the other side of the field was a steep rock wall, the head of the ravine. Tucked in the corner, barely visible in the rain, was a neat stone hut. Shelter from the storm. I walked over and climbed stairs around the back of the hut. At the top was a very low timber door. I drew a wooden latch and pushed. The door popped open. The hut smelt of damp earth and burnt wood. In the half-light, I made out a table with benches on either side and a fireplace with logs set. Opposite this was a kitchen bench with pots and pans dangling from the hooks above it. In the far corner was a bedframe strung with woven cord. A thin mattress was rolled up beside it. Above the bed, pinned to the rafter, was a page torn from a notebook, with a message handwritten in biro: *O Viandante che Tu Passi, Mangia e Bevi Ma non Lasciare Segni di Sporcizzia. Un Grazzie (sic) del Pastore Diddio.* With this elegant note, the owner had given me permission to use the little hut, but kindly asked for it to be cleaned up afterwards. *Oh Wayfarer who passes,*

Eat and Drink But don't Leave a Mess. With the Thankks (sic)
of Cowherd Diddio.

I sat down at the table, fished an energy bar out of the side of my pack, and listened to the rain beating on the roof, thinking how nice it would be to light the fire and rest in this warm cocoon. This was not to be though, maybe the next time. I prepared myself properly for the next leg. I took my glasses off and stowed them in the bag; they were less than useless in the wet. I also fished out my pair of plastic rain pants and squirmed into them, banging my head on one of the beams. I adjusted the cover on the pack, swung it onto my back and zipped up my jacket. I straightened the chair and pulled the hood over my head. I silently thanked Diddio for his hospitality and stepped back out into the rain, feeling well sorted, even cocky. As someone once said, there is no such thing as bad weather, just bad gear.

While I was in the hut, the meadow had been engulfed by mist and rain. The head of the Mologna Ravine was a vast amphitheatre of glacial rubble that had collapsed from the cliffs that towered above it, an arc of scree and rocks, but this was completely hidden from me under the low clouds. The Rifugio Rivetti was tucked under one of these cliffs, somewhere up there high above me, distant and invisible. I knew I still had the hardest couple of hours in front of me, but I felt ready for it now.

I started back up the trail; I could see nothing above me,

nor could I see the valley below. Head down, I concentrated on the greasy rocks I was stepping on. Ten minutes after leaving Diddio's hut, a sudden rush of cold air descended on me. I looked up into the clouds and then continued my climb. The cold air came again. I jammed down my hat and kept going. The rain began to fall more heavily, and the clouds started to swirl. I thought about returning to the hut but there wasn't time, so I took off my pack – the electronics and metal would have attracted lightning – lay it on the ground and then left the trail, walking carefully through the scrub to an overhang that seemed to offer some protection, and pressed in against the wall.

The electrical storm then broke with all its fury. The thunder was simultaneous with the flashes of lightning, short and sharp, like the noise of a door slamming, but multiplied a thousand-fold. It reverberated off the peaks and cliffs above me and rolled down the valley. It seemed like I was the very focus of the storm. I felt that the mountain was shouting at me. Warning me off. Telling me I didn't belong there. I crouched lower, hugging myself, leaning harder into the wall. Not praying, but almost. And then it stopped, as quickly as it had started. The wind had changed to the north-west, and the rain started to subside, turning into a steady drizzle, but I stayed where I was for another five minutes, reluctant to leave my shelter until I was sure the coast was clear. I stood up, stretched, swept off the dirt and bracken that had stuck to my jacket, and looked around me. I walked over to the trail, avoiding the puddles and the rivulets that were running off the rocks. I picked up my pack, hooked it onto my back and started back up the trail, shaken but undeterred.

And so it went for the next hour, a relentless ascent following a narrow path under granite crags until finally, almost gasping for breath, I came to a crossroad of paths beside the ruins of a stone hut. Near the hut was a stake with three signs fixed to it. They pointed in three different directions: one pointed back down the ravine from where I had come, Piedicavallo, two and a half hours away; another pointed to Colle della Bosa and the Rifugio La Vecchia Lago to the left, three and a half hours away; and the third, hallelujah, pointed to Rifugio Rivetti up to the right, only thirty minutes further on.

It turned out to be the longest half-hour of my life. I was exhausted. I had to stop every 20 metres or so, bend over, hands on my knees, staring at the ground, trying to rally the energy for the next 20 metres. Periodically, the trail would level out, promising the end of the climb, only to reveal another rise through the mist. After fifteen minutes or so, suddenly, as if to reward the efforts I had made, the clouds parted for an instant, and there, sitting on a bluff gazing out across the valley, was the Rifugio Rivetti, a majestic, tall stone building with a red roof. The clouds quickly closed in again and the *rifugio* disappeared, but the sight had been enough to spur me on, to carry me over the line.

With one last push, I finally arrived, slipping down a rock path to the clearing at the entrance to the building. I leant against a stone wall and vomited, glad that there was no one outside to witness it and glad that the heavy rain was carrying away the partially digested tortellini. I rinsed my mouth, then walked over to a stone bench beside the door and slowly unlaced my boots. I pushed the door open and entered a vestibule, a wet room lined with racks crowded with sodden hiking boots. Above this was a row of hooks dripping with raincoats. I added mine to the piles, found a pair of Crocs that fitted me more-or-less and shuffled through a second door, stepping into the warmth of the *rifugio*, greeted by ironic clapping from lazy hikers who had probably witnessed my arrival through the frosted windows. Unable to speak, I smiled back, bowed my head and lowered myself onto a bench near the fire.

A young woman came out of the kitchen, walked over and welcomed me to the Rifugio Rivetti. I ordered *una birra grande e un tagliere di affettati e formaggi* not because I wanted them, I knew a large mug of tea would have been better on my delicate stomach, but because this had been the reward that had kept me grinding up the trail in the rain. Several minutes later, a large bottle of Menabrea was placed in front of me. This was followed by a wooden board with artfully arranged slices of salami and cheeses and a basket of bread and grissini. I sipped on the beer, chewed a bread stick and looked around me.

I was sitting under a dog-eared hiking map, pinned to the wall like a butterfly. It was covered in networks of trails highlighted in red texta, which had been worn thin by the countless fingers that had tracked along them. The rest of the walls in the room were crowded with shelves crammed with books and old bottles and crooked frames with faded black-and-white photos of snow-covered peaks and mountaineers long gone.

The *rifugio* had been there for one hundred years, in one version or another. It had a fraught history. It was commissioned in 1909 by the local branch of the Club Alpino Italiano to encourage hikers and climbers into this little-known corner of the mountains. The club received additional funding from the Rivetti family, textile industrialists from Biella, to commemorate their son Alfredo who had been swept away by an avalanche in these parts in 1911. World War I intervened and the new *rifugio* wasn't inaugurated until July 1921. In 1925, it was seriously damaged by another avalanche. It was hit a second time in 1928. Undeterred, doubtless emboldened by the challenge, the local Fascist mayor oversaw the construction of snow barriers up high under the cliffs and commissioned a third edition of the *rifugio*. Rivetti, version 3, was inaugurated with great pomp in 1935. One thousand people were reported to have climbed up here for the event, on foot or carried by donkeys. The mayor made a lengthy speech. Afterwards, a crowd climbed up to the ridge, the Passo della Mologna Grande, where a memorial to soldiers lost in World War I was commemorated and a wreath of flowers was laid in memory of Alfredo Rivetti. They then re-joined the others at the *rifugio*, where they had a picnic lunch on the surrounding meadows before returning to the valley. They certainly were better people than me. The contractors must have done a good job with the barriers because the *rifugio* has been here, unmolested, ever since. It would have been here when Carl and his mates climbed up the valley, but he made no mention of it.

Revived by the beer and snacks, I pushed myself off the bench and walked shakily over to the kitchen to check in. The narrow galley was crowded with people toiling over bubbling cauldrons. A short woman with perfect English turned to me.

'Oh, you are the Owstaraliano. Sandrooo!' she shouted without taking her eyes off me, placing stress heavily on the last syllable. 'Sandrooo!'

A tall, rangy middle-aged man wearing shorts, a loose T-shirt and a snood pulled low over his forehead loped in from outside. 'Ah, l'Owstraliano!' he shouted at me, extending his long, sinewy arm. '*Benvenuto. Benvenuto.*'

Sandro cleared a space on a bench, took out an old exercise book and I wrote my name on a stained page. Booking a place here wasn't essential but it was appreciated. They were obliged to take in whoever turned up, whenever. It wasn't possible to turn someone away on a cold, wet night when the nearest alternative was a hard three-hour walk away. In busy periods this may mean rolling out a mattress on the messroom floor. Fortunately, not this night.

I had been allocated a place in the sleeping zone on the top floor. I manoeuvred my pack up a very steep flight of stairs, the shallow treads rounded by years of use, past dormitories to the second floor, a long, cavernous space under a pitched roof, with a single window at the far end. Mattresses were lined cheek by jowl down either side. There was a heavy blanket and a pillow neatly folded on each mattress and a bench at the foot of the mattress where we could stow our packs. Washing was dripping from lines stretched between the beams. The two window spaces were already taken so I picked a mattress near the stairs so I could creep down to the toilet in the middle of the night without disturbing anyone.

I sorted my things, took out a change of clothes and headed down to the bathroom, of which there was only one, a small room with a hole-in-the-ground toilet and a shower head protruding out of the tiled wall above it. Quite a challenge but I managed to undress without taking my

Crocs off, wash myself and the day's clothes under the drizzling shower and get dressed in the fresh clothes, still in my Crocs, all without incident. Backing out of the tiny cubicle, I felt like a million bucks and my appetite was back, teased by the delicious aromas wafting out of the kitchen.

The tables in the dining room had been arranged around the walls, refectory style. I was one of the last to sit down. There was a low buzz of conversation and about twenty or so people were spread out, waiting happily for their dinner. I sat in the middle of a long table, with a young German couple in front of me and an older Swiss couple on my right. We introduced ourselves and shook hands and they politely switched from speaking German to English.

'Sydney?' Christophe exclaimed in his slow, musical Swiss accent. 'I love Sydney. I worked there for Rupert Murdoch. Well, I did not actually meet him but my company installed News Corp's colour printing presses at Chullora. We lived in Concord. We loved it. Absolutely loved it.'

Sandro, dressed in an apron, carried a huge pot out of the kitchen, placed it on a table in the middle of the room and began ladling large serves of pasta into deep bowls which his staff delivered to our tables: rigatoni with a meat sauce and plenty of parmesan cheese sprinkled on top. It was a very convivial evening. I was an oddity in the room: the only non-European and the only English-speaker; the rest were German, Swiss and Italian.

The Grande Traversata delle Alpi, the GTA, is a 1000-kilometre marked trail which starts at Molini di Calasca on the Swiss–Italian border and heads south, finishing at Ventimiglia on the Mediterranean coast. If you go straight through, it takes sixty days, fifty-nine stages. Rifugio Rivetti is stage 27. The most common way of doing the hike is a week at a time, year after year, working your way down the range to the coast. This was how the people I talked with were doing it, although there was one person, a surly old German gentleman with a ruddy face sitting alone in the corner, who was doing the whole route, end to end, on his own, in one go.

'Please tell me,' said Dieter on my right, 'what brings an Australian to these European mountains? It is a long way from home.'

I told my neighbours my story, in English for a change, with other people listening in. It was a little awkward. I didn't embellish the nasty bits and we managed to skip over the details of the Nazi occupation with a few laughs and shrugs, water well under the bridge.

'By the way, you do know that you are walking in the wrong direction?' piped up Kerri, the Swiss lady sitting in front of me. Everyone laughed.

'No, I did not know that,' I replied, a little surprised.

'Yes!' she declared, leaning forward. 'You should be doing it from north to south, like everyone else.' She sat back.

Everyone agreed. 'You should start in the mountains and then you should walk to the sea. Downhill all the way. It's logical. You know what the Swiss are like. I'm sure if you get there, they'll probably fine you. They'll certainly turn you around. If not, they will make you walk backwards!' She laughed but I wasn't sure if she was joking or not.

The main course was a beef stew with vegetables and a coleslaw salad. Once the dinner had been served, Sandro and his team slid in at the end of the table and joined us for the meal. Glasses were filled and the crew were toasted.

'*Allora*,' Sandro said, raising his glass towards me. '*Caro Australiano*, what brings you here?'

I took a deep breath and a sip of wine, and I told my story once more, the Uncle John version. It was becoming something of a recital for me, and I knew my lines well. I knew when to pause for a laugh and when to pause for reflection. My Italian had become more fluent with every retelling. I had the vocabulary down pat, idioms rolled off my tongue with ease; and I even ventured into the subjunctive mood. I felt it had become something of a virtuoso performance.

Once I'd finished, Massimo, Sandro's fifteen-year-old son who was up here helping for the summer, piped up excitedly. 'Papa! Papa!' He prodded his father. 'Tell him about Giuseppe.'

'Sure,' said Sandro, not needing much encouragement, 'but first we'll need some more wine.'

The story Sandro told me involved three men. The first two were Harry Miller, from Perth, Western Australia; and Frank Bowes, from Christchurch, New Zealand; both escapees from Campo 106 in Vercelli in September 1943. The third person was Giuseppe Paschetto, Massimo's maths and science teacher from the secondary school of Mosso, a small town in the mountains above Biella.

Harry Miller was born in Birmingham in 1920 and enlisted to serve in the AIF in April 1941. Frank Bowes was born in Christchurch in 1907 and enlisted in the New Zealand army in 1940. Both men were taken prisoner in El-Alamein in 1943, served time in Grupignano and Vercelli, before escaping on 8 September 1943. In the mountains they met Francesco Crestani, a young deserter. Unlike most of their colleagues who made their way towards freedom in Switzerland, the two Anzacs decided to join Crestani's fledgling partisan group 'Piave', a detachment of the Garibaldi brigade. It had its base in the mountains above Mosso in an abandoned mountain lodge known as the 'baita di Basto'. They belonged to the Lupo, or Wolf, unit. By autumn, the detachment had increased to seventy-five volunteers, and the battle-hardened Anzacs were a great asset to the force. They carried out raids and sabotages throughout the area, disrupting the enemy forces.

On 17 February, the partisans did a sweep through the surrounding area, rounding up spies and collaborators, losing several of their leaders in the action. The following day, the twelve presumed spies, seven men and five women, were executed against the walls of the church of the Santa Liberata, outside Mosso cemetery. Amongst the victims were Gemma Botta, twenty-one years old; her sister Duilia Botta, twenty-three years old; and their father, Carlo Botta, fifty-nine years old.

Two days later, on 20 February, the Fascist and German forces retaliated. Most of the Detachment Piave managed to escape to the neighbouring valley, the Valsessera; however, the Wolf unit was surrounded and overwhelmed. The nine survivors, several of whom were still teenagers, were taken to the Fascist headquarters at the town of Pray. One partisan, Vincenzo Lazzarotto, was summarily shot there. Another, a woman called Iris Paride, was spared and eventually sent to a concentration camp in Germany.

The following day, the remaining seven partisans, including Frank and Harry, were taken to the church of Santa Liberata above Mosso and lined up against the same wall where the twelve spies had been executed two days earlier; and, at 1.00 pm on 21 February 1944, were machine-gunned to death. Had Harry and Frank participated in the terrible event two days previously? They were, after all, amongst the oldest and most experienced of the unit. Did they think of it when it was their turn to face the firing squad? With the killing of the seven partisans, revenge was fulfilled, for now. An eye for an eye. A tooth for a tooth. And so it went for another two terrible years.

Giuseppe Paschetto, the third person in the story, worked at the high school in Mosso, the Vittorio Sella Alpine School of Peace, until 2020. It is a modest school with considerable ambitions dedicated to the values of mountaineering (Vittorio Sella was a historic, local Alpinist) and to peace. In 2008, Paschetto and some colleagues, including Agostino Costenaro, decided to turn these terrible events in their town's history to good. They imagined that the students at the schools that Harry and Frank attended would have had no idea about these young men's stories. Wouldn't it be great, they thought, to get in touch with the schools to explain how Harry and Frank had given their lives in these mountains for the freedom of all and to express their community's gratitude.

The teachers believed that it was important to transmit to their students the values of courage, generosity, altruism and the love of liberty that inspired Frank and Harry to join the partisans of the Valle Mosso and fight Nazism, rather than escaping to safety in Switzerland.

After the initial research, the teachers decided to focus on Frank. The year-long project, involving Year 10 students from the middle school, resulted in, among other things, the establishment of a permanent research unit at the school dedicated to the history of the twentieth century and the war of liberation; the creation of a short feature film based on Frank's life, scripted, directed, scored, filmed and acted by the students and teachers of the school; the development of a hiking trail that linked the different locations of the story; and the visit of a delegation of nine students and five teachers to Christchurch, where they were hosted by Frank's old school, Christchurch Boys High School. The highlight of the project was when Frank's son, who was born on the day that Frank left New Zealand for the war in Europe, visited Mosso and the surrounding area for two weeks as a guest of the school, arriving on 23 April 2011.

~~~

We went through two carafes of wine while Sandro told his story. After everyone had returned to the meal, I asked Sandro about his life up here at the Rifugio Rivetti.

'It's tough,' he said, 'but I love it. I've been manager here for more than twenty years, but it is something I couldn't do without these guys.' He pointed at his colleagues Claudia and Ales, both students up here for the summer, and to Massimo, who smiled proudly back at us. 'They are the first up in the morning and the last to bed at night.'

He explained that the *rifugio* is open from June to

September. All the heavy stuff – oil, flour, beer, wine and fuel – is brought up by helicopter at the start of the season.

'You have to order well,' he said, 'because that's it for the summer. We make our bread and pastries and sometimes pasta up here, if we have time. But for anything fresh, like fruit and vegetables,' he pointed again to his colleagues, 'they have to go all the way down on foot and pick it up from Piedicavallo and bring it all back up here.' I groaned. He shrugged. 'They are young. It's good for them.'

'You know we have an annual race here?' he said proudly. 'From Piedicavallo to the *rifugio*. Every year, the first Sunday of September. It kind of closes off the season for us. I used to do it myself.' I could imagine him, with his long rangy limbs, trotting up the rocky path. 'But I'm too old now. Too hard. Still, we had nearly one hundred competitors last year. Men and women. The record is forty-eight minutes from bottom to top.' I shook my head and slumped back in my seat, exhausted at the thought of it.

The meal finished with a generous bowl of *bunet* pudding. As the coffee arrived, Sandro took several bottles down from the shelves and placed them along the tables. They each had a hand-drawn label, Goofy in a large yellow hat holding a bottle: GRAPPA ACHILLEA, grappa steeped with dried yarrow flowers. We toasted Sandro and his staff again and sculled the burning liquid, exactly what you want from a true mountain grappa.

Everyone helped clear the plates and glasses and reset the tables for breakfast. We were now allowed to bring our boots in from the cold and crowd them around the stove so they would be dry for the morning. It was early, only nine o'clock, but once dinner had been sorted and breakfast laid out, the generator was turned off, the lights went out and it was time for bed.

I waited, chatting with Sandro until the others had gone up. After one more shot of grappa, I said goodnight to the crew and climbed the stairs, now in total darkness. I managed to weave my way through the low hanging washing and wriggle into my cotton sleeping sack without touching my neighbours, who lay still on either side.

Above: A light snack at the Rifugio Rivetti.

Below: The village of Rosazza in the Valle Cervo.

Above: Alpeggio Maccagno in Valle Vogna,
the highest cheesemaker in the Alps.

Below: Valle Vogna, hiking towards Sant'Antonio.

CHAPTER 5

Rifugio Rivetti to Sant'Antonio
16 kilometres, 1400-metre ascent, 7.5 hours

Dawn had barely broken when the first keen hikers started whispering. It was my turn to feign sleep, waiting until everyone had dressed and then headed downstairs, trailing their packs behind them. I lay still with my eyes closed, listening to the rain falling on the roof. When the last person had left, I walked to the window and peered out. There was a grey light, the black silhouettes of the mountains to the south were just visible on the horizon. Water trickled down the windowpane. No point in waiting, I thought, this rain wasn't going to go away and I had a long day ahead of me.

I had a large bowl of cereal and a couple of slices of stale bread with butter and jam for breakfast. I pulled on my boots, nice and toasty from the fire, and positioned my pack at the door. Sandro had prepared the usual panini, cheese and ham, which I stowed in the top of my pack along with an apple and two bars of hikers' chocolate. I leant into the kitchen and said goodbye to the staff, shook Sandro's hand, assured him I'd be back soon and left the building.

The rain had lightened to a drizzle and the clouds were lifting but the ridge was still barely visible, a grey wall under a white mantle. The path zigzagged up into the clouds. I had to use clumps of spiny grass for handholds to leverage myself over the boulders. I had twinges in both my knees but nothing serious. Despite the snoring and farts in the dormitory, I had slept well and felt refreshed, even looking forward to the challenge.

Twenty minutes after leaving the *rifugio*, I was at the top, the Passo della Mologna Grande, a rocky saddle between two peaks. It was marked by a tall cairn with fading walking signs painted on the side and a string of ragged Tibetan flags. The clouds had cleared. Far below was the *rifugio*, a tiny rectangle balanced on the edge of a precipice, ready to tumble into the sea of mist that still filled the valley below. Lines of jagged ridges emerged from the mist, disappearing in layers like a Chinese landscape.

The peak on my right was called Punta Tre Vescovi, the peak of the three bishops. It has this curious name because it is the point where three valleys converge: Valle Cervo, Valle del Lys and the Valsesia, respectively the dioceses of Vercelli, Aosta and Novara. This remote crest had been an unlikely point of transit for migrants, petty traders, refugees and escapees, an ancient link between the German speakers to the north, French speakers to the west and Italian speakers to the south. I headed north, towards the Valsesia.

Once over the ridge, I was greeted by a sight of almost lunar desolation. The ridge fell away to a sea of rubble, a vast moraine of striated blocks and boulders, the remnants of long-gone glaciers. At a distance, the path was well camouflaged, flat stones dragged into place, almost invisible amongst the wreckage except for occasional yellow markers and small cairns a metre or so high that stood guard at strategic points. These were known as *ometti* in Italian, little men. I slipped and slid down the muddy track and disappeared into the debris.

On the other side of the moraine, the path took a long climb up the side of a grassy slope. The clouds and mist had risen and there were even flashes of blue in the sky. I could look down to the left over the grasslands and pine forests into the deep Valle del Lys, the homonymous river snaking along the valley floor far below.

Two hours after leaving the *rifugio*, I came up to the Colle Lazouney, the second pass of the day. It was less impressive than the first one, a narrow gap between low rocks that I wouldn't have noticed if I hadn't seen a sign fixed to one of the boulders. Time for a break. I had a long drink of water and chewed on a row of chocolate.

I looked around and marvelled. Here I was sitting on a rock by myself high in the Alps, not another soul around, sucking on a piece of chocolate as if it was the most natural thing to be doing and then, for a couple of seconds, I was completely disoriented. It was one of those moments where reality crashes into the present and you have to take a little time out and ask yourself, well, how did I get here?

~

My love affair with Italy wasn't always a done deal. My first contact was stepping onto a poorly lit wharf in Brindisi on a cold, drizzling January evening in 1980. To a generation of backpackers before me, Brindisi was the wrong end of the world. This was probably a little unfair as they generally only experienced the squalid stretch of road connecting the port with the railway station, a transition point between the islands of Greece and the fleshpots of western Europe.

I didn't see anything to contradict this opinion as I dragged my Gladstone bag towards the trains myself, although I was impressed along the way when observing through a window a *piazzaiolo* spinning a disc of creamy dough around the tip of his finger like a Chinese acrobat before slapping it on a table, raising a cloud of flour.

I found a window seat in a crowded second-class carriage and settled in for the long trip to the Straits of Messina and the island of Sicily. Although only young, I was already a dogmatic traveller, something of a travel snob. I wasn't planning on spending much time in Italy, too touristy. I avoided Greece for the same reason. Instead, I was heading to Malta, where I planned to spend my six months abroad, writing and absorbing authentic local life. It didn't work out.

Arriving in Reggio Calabria the next morning, I took the ferry across the Straits of Messina. The only youth hostel open in the middle of winter was in Castroreale, a hilltop village 10 kilometres west of Messina. I took the train to Barcellona (the Sicilian version has two l's). While waiting in the station bar for the bus to Castroreale, I was surrounded by a group of young guys who were keen to practise their English. As I left to board the bus, they shook my hand and slipped me a couple of joints.

It took almost an hour, leaving the scruffy sprawl, twisting up narrow roads past olive groves and allotments to get to Castroreale, a walled village on the top of a steep hill, barely visible beneath the low clouds. The bus dropped me off in the main square, then did an awkward three-point turn and headed back down the hill. I stood alone, shivering in the square until I spotted an arrow with 'Ostello' and followed its directions uphill to the castle. As I stood perplexed at the entrance, an old lady approached me. She signalled to wait and then hurried downhill. Ten minutes later she returned with a large key.

She put the key in the great wooden door and pushed it open, leading me across a dark vestibule, up two flights of stairs and down an even darker corridor that was painted in the shiny creams and browns of a hospital. At the end was a dormitory with three double bunks. Next to the dorm was a bathroom with rows of deep sinks and shower vestibules and then a kitchen. I put my bag on a bed and followed the lady back down to the entrance, our footsteps echoing in the half light.

She let me know there was no breakfast nor was there a restaurant in town. She pointed down the hill and repeated 'alimentare' with a wave of her hand. She helped herself to 20,000 lira from my opened wallet and showed me where to leave the key when I left. She shook my hand and headed off down the hill, leaving me alone in my very own castle.

I closed the door and followed her down the hill, stocking up on provisions at the *alimentare* – some bread, a couple of tomatoes, local hard cheese, a bar of chocolate and a bottle of red wine – and returned to base. I tried to explore further but the doors were locked. I climbed on the bed and peered through the bars on the window but all I saw was down into a dark alley. There was no heating, so I put on another layer of clothing, poured a glass of wine, rolled a cigarette and lay on my bed reading until darkness fell. I went down to the kitchen, prepared my dinner, sat at a table and kept reading while I chewed on the bread and victuals.

By the time I had finished the meal, I was mostly through the wine and decided, what the hell, I might as well smoke one of those joints, which proved to be not one of my wiser decisions. The weather had closed in, the kitchen curtains billowed and heavy rain pounded the roof. It was too cold to shower or even get changed so I pulled on an extra layer of clothes, poured the last of the wine, lay on the bed under a pile of mouldy blankets with my torch and a book, and waited as the marijuana-induced anxiety crept over me. The wind picked up, scratching branches across the windows and rattling chains outside. It was the beginning of one of the most harrowing and uncomfortable nights of my life. By the time the sun had risen, I was packed and heading downhill to the bus stop.

Overnight my plans had changed. The idea of sitting on my contemplative own on a Mediterranean island in winter had lost its appeal. A city boy at heart, with some relief, I had decided to head north to Rome hoping my Italian experience would improve.

I took the bus back to Barcellona and then the slow train from Messina up to Rome, sitting on a dickie chair in the crowded corridor, smoking cigarettes and watching the sparkling rocky bays of Calabria slip by. Eight hours later I arrived at Roma Termini station. I threw my bag down from the carriage, ignored the porters and followed my fellow travellers along the platform and into the towering concourse. I was impressed by the number of police with machine guns slung over their shoulders patrolling the station. 1980 was a turbulent time in Italy – the mafia wars were in full swing in Sicily and *gli anni di piombo*, the 'years of lead', the struggle between far left and far right terrorism, was unravelling in the north of the country.

A middle-aged lady waiting outside rounded up me and a few other backpackers and walked us from the station to a third-floor *pensione* in a seedy nearby street. I had teamed up with an American guy I had met on the train. We were young and very excited to be in Rome, Caput Mundi, the capital of the world. We were also naive and pretty dumb, although I didn't learn this until several hours later as we were attempting to get up the stairs to our building, having drunk a lot of cheap wine in the bar opposite.

I had peeled off a wad of lira and, in a final flourish of drunken gratitude to the people of this great city, I shouted the whole bar drinks before heading back to the *pensione*. Two of our newfound friends kindly accompanied us across the street and helped us negotiate the stairs to our accommodation, lifting my wallet from my back pocket as they did so and then sprinting off down the poorly lit street. I took offence and ran after them, the sides of the street rolling with each step. Unfortunately, I caught them two blocks later – at least I thought it was them. I was so drunk that I wasn't expecting the inevitable: a punch in the mouth delivered like the hammer of Thor, which pretty much finished my evening, although not my assailant's. I slumped back against a car and tried to cover up as he continued to land a series of easy punches. A voice inside me suggested that if I dropped to the ground, he'd stop hitting me. It wasn't a great plan, but it was the only one I could come up with and, happily, it worked.

I watched as four boots disappeared down the wet footpath, and then pulled myself up and leant against the car. Several people came and fussed over me. A lady gave me a handful of tissues to mop up the blood from my mouth and nose and a young guy helped me make my way back to the stairs where the drunken Texan was waiting.

Our host, a motherly lady, was beside herself. She took me into the bathroom and patched me up. After I had vomited several times, she led me back to my bed, where I lay more or less in a coma for that night and most of the next day. Fortunately, even in my sorry state, I didn't blame the Italians. I concluded that it was my own fault. It could have happened anywhere.

I say fortunately, because I was able to shrug off the assault quickly and begin to appreciate the area where I was staying. I even became a regular at the bar across the road. In fact, I settled right in. In those days, there weren't many guidebooks around. Before I left home, I had been given the *Michelin Green Guide to Italy*, a tall slim volume with elegant sketches of the Leaning Tower of Pisa, the Colosseum and a happy girl in a Fiat 500 on the cover. The descriptions were essential, never more than a paragraph or two, often accompanied by more elegant little sketches. There were handy maps, fundamental in a pre-Google world. The sites were arranged alphabetically, rated by stars, which made it easy to plan my days. With the guide stuffed in my back pocket, I spent the next month exploring Rome, not just the sites but also the life in the piazzas and streets that surrounded them. Italy was working its magic but it wasn't until I met Andres that I really fell unequivocally in love with the country.

Being a long-term resident in the *pensione*, the *signora* upgraded me from the group dormitory to a two-bed room with a balcony. I returned to my room late one afternoon to find a large guy about the same age as me lying on the other bed with his hands behind his head, looking up at the ceiling. When I came in, he jumped up, shook my hand and introduced himself in a soft Dutch drawl, Andres from Hilversum. He was big and tall, with thick dark hair and a handsome, friendly face; overall, not unlike Michelangelo's statue of David.

He was also a nice guy. Not the sharpest pencil in the box, but he was quiet and friendly. That evening, we went out to get a pizza and beer together. He told me he came to Italy a couple of times a year but he wasn't interested in coming out with me the next morning to EUR to check out the Fascist architecture. Why did he come so regularly to Italy, I enquired? To fuck Italian girls, he replied succinctly, without looking up from his pizza. Fair enough, I thought. It wasn't as if I hadn't noticed how beautiful Italian girls were, but I had never dared to think that I could even talk with one.

Two days later, I left Rome and headed north to Florence, Andres tagging along. It was in Florence that I got to admire his style. The first night there he suggested we go to a disco. It was the early 1980s, disco was king but I had cut my teeth on punk and indie music performed in grotty inner-city pubs where the carpet stuck to your shoes, and I had never actually been into a disco. But what the hell, I thought, this is Italy. We put on our best threads and headed out into the Florentine evening.

It was mid-February, full winter. It was bitterly cold and dark. The cobbled streets shone with rain, reflecting the colours of the streetlights and neon signs. Although it was late, the footpaths were still crowded with people dressed in overcoats, furs and Moncler ski jackets, all trying to keep out of the rain. We had a cheap dinner and then Andres led the way to my first disco, which had a discreet sign pointing down a steep flight of stairs. Although we surely didn't meet the dress code, they still let us in, probably because we were foreigners, which was a novelty in those days.

Andres' strategy was simple. He ordered the drinks and we sat at the bar and waited. It worked like a charm. Before long, two very attractive girls sidled up to us – well, sidled up to him – and began talking. We spent some time together, even hitting the dance floor, but at a certain point the girls said they had to go home, shook our hands, pecked us on the cheeks and left the bar. It was a disappointing end but I was still impressed. It was the first time I had even spoken to an Italian girl.

The following evening, we went out with two English girls who were staying at the *pensione*. It was a more relaxed evening. We made merry, pub-crawling some of the less fancy establishments and drank far too much, rousing our host at an ungodly hour. The following night we went out again. As we left the *pensione*, our host warned us to be back by eleven or he would lock us out. The evening was a reprise of the one before and we staggered up the lane to the *pensione* well after midnight. When we rang the buzzer, our host did not answer. We tried again, and again – still no answer. A light snow had started to fall but we were drunk enough to laugh it off and teeter back down the lane without a fixed plan. Before we got to the end of the lane, Andres and one of the girls announced they were going to find a hotel, walking away holding hands. The other girl and I looked at each other awkwardly. We silently negotiated that nothing was going to happen, smiled at each other with relief, buttoned our coats and started walking.

All the squares and buildings were still lit, everything was covered with a light dust of snow, and there wasn't a single other person about. The most beautiful city in the world was ours. After a couple of hours of roaming, the cold got the better of us and we walked to Santa Maria Novella railway station and took refuge in the heated waiting room, along with the other homeless and weary, dozing fitfully, cuddled together in very uncomfortable seats.

When the sun rose, the city began to wake up. In the enchanting half-light, we left the station and headed towards the Mercato Comunale. We wandered through the halls avoiding trucks and trolleys, admiring the spectacular produce that was being laid out in the stalls and recoiling from the bloody butchers' displays with their dangling sides of venison and wild boar, fur and innards still attached, and the sad trays packed with neat rows of endangered birds.

On the other side of the market, we found a smoke-filled bar that was open for business. We pushed our way through a layer of burly men and ordered a cappuccino and ham and cheese croissant each. We bellied up to the far end of the bar and gazed through the misted window at the activity outside. I was grateful that we had been locked out and that Andres had abandoned us. It had been a perfect evening and I had fallen in love with Italy. Hook, line and sinker.

Recalibrated and refreshed, I finished my row of chocolate, slung on my pack and continued on my way down through the Colle Lazouney. Beyond the pass, the path dropped to a broad swampy field. Beyond this was a dry riverbed and then a high wall of stone that ran east–west behind it. I squelched down the hill to a tall cairn with a number of walking signs fixed on it. With little thought, I followed the most prominent sign and turned left, pleased to be walking downhill on a wide easy path through green pastures. I heard dogs barking in the distance and came over a rise to see a flock of a hundred or so sheep, pearly white grubs grazing on the lush green grass. The barking got louder as I got closer. As I approached the flock, I spotted three snarling white Maremmano dogs, their loose, woolly fur a perfect disguise amongst the sheep. Opposite, a tarpaulin was stretched between two large rocks and secured by ropes, the shepherd's bivouac.

I was taking a couple of photos when I noticed a man in a dark jacket, with a woollen cap and an umbrella folded under his arm, walking slowly up the hill towards me. The dogs stopped barking, standing down to greet him. I think he was more surprised to see me than I was to see him. He placed his small backpack on a rock and shook my hand.

'What, may I ask, brings you to these remote parts?' he said, smiling through a grey goatee. I told him an abbreviated version of my story, no time for trimmings this morning. He nodded as I spoke and told me that he had heard such stories before. He was interested in Australia. He asked me how the economy was going, as several young people from his valley had gone to study and work there. He was clearly up for a chat, so I asked him about the sheep.

'I'm a *magaro*, a shepherd,' he told me. 'I have done this work all my life, like my father and my grandfather.' He rotated his open hand slowly to indicate an unbroken line that probably went back centuries. 'But I think I'll probably be the last. The last *magaro* of the Valle del Lys,' he added, smiling at the thought. 'My children all have jobs in the valley and I doubt any of my grandchildren will follow me up here. Why would they? There are too many opportunities elsewhere.' I wasn't so sure about that. I had heard that there were a lot of young Italians who were turning their backs on the disappointments of the cities and moving up into the mountains, restoring abandoned family houses and reviving old trades.

He told me that the flock was Sambuca sheep, a local breed raised for their meat. 'I come up here twice a week to feed the dogs and move the pens. I walk them up at the beginning of summer, usually around the beginning of June or maybe a bit earlier, it depends, and then take them back down before winter starts.' He laughed. 'There used to be a big fanfare when we left the village; bonfires, torches lighting the way. The whole village would come out to wish us well, it wasn't just me back then. The same thing when we brought the flocks back down. Now,' he smiled, 'they couldn't give a stuff. Everyone's inside by the fire watching their screens. By the way, where are you headed?'

'Sant'Antonio in the Valle Vogna,' I told him.

He raised his eyebrows in surprise. 'Just as well I asked.' He took me by the arm and turned me around. 'You are going the wrong way, my friend.'

Turns out I was heading west down the Valle Loos towards the Valle del Lys rather than north over the Maccagno Pass towards the Valle Vogna. I had taken the wrong turn at the swamp, unconsciously choosing the easier option. We both laughed and I thanked him. We shook hands and I climbed back up the hill. 'Auguri!' he called out before turning back to his dogs.

I returned to the swamp. Fortunately, I hadn't lost much time. I now saw the smaller yellow sign that pointed north across the field to the vertical wall of stone at the top of which was the Passo del Maccagno, the third pass of the day. Once over this, it would be a long descent, four or five hours, down the Valle Vogna to Sant'Antonio, where I was spending the night.

A well-worn path led me across the swamp and the dry creek bed and then got lost in the rubble and scree at the base of the climb. Once above the scree, the path steepened, tacking through thick tussocks and rocks, its muddy surface as slippery as ice. Halfway up, I stopped to catch my breath and turned around, impressed by the height I had gained so quickly. I looked back down over the empty creek bed and the boggy meadows to the saw-toothed ridges in the south.

I used my toes, knees and elbows to grind my way to the top, anchoring myself to tussocks with my free hand, feeling that if I let go, the weight of my backpack would pull me off the mountain and I would tumble back into the valley far below. Finally at the top, I needed one last push to drag myself over the lip, belly first. I lay panting on a large flat rock, the Passo del Maccagno.

It was quiet and cold. I lay still for several minutes, my cheek resting on the damp stone, feeling a gentle breeze passing over me. I crawled away from the edge, sat up, threw off my backpack, struggled to my feet and looked around. A faded sign painted on a rock told me that the Passo del Maccagno is 2495 metres above sea level, the highest point of the day. I was standing on the edge of two worlds: behind me the high plains and rocky folds of the Valle d'Aosta; in front of me the cramped, dark gorges of Piedmont.

I was standing on the rim of another glacial valley, the Valle Vogna. It had been gouged empty by glaciers, which had left behind a shell, a rim of streaked black cliffs that dropped hundreds of metres into the valley. At the bottom, there was a small black lake, half hidden behind a bluff. The view was no cheerier further north, a landscape of boulders and ravines stretching all the way to the Corno Bianco. Behind this peak, I caught my first glimpse of Monte Rosa breaking through thick clouds.

I had a long suck on my CamelBak and ate the last of the chocolate. I then reloaded the backpack and headed down into the valley, scrambling over a jumble of boulders. It was a long, tricky descent, hopping from wet rock to wet rock, crossing and recrossing a tumbling stream until I reached the bottom and stood on the shore of Lago Nero. A herd of big, black cows grazing peacefully on the slopes above the lake ignored me, their large bronze bells clanging slowly around their necks.

The trail, now well worn by generations of cattle and lined by rocks splattered with cow pats, wound downhill, following the side of the stream. The rain had set in again, moving from a light drizzle to a steady drumming on the hood of my raincoat. The mountain peaks disappeared under clouds once more. I had been walking for nearly four hours. My glasses were misty. I was cold and tired. I passed more cows and a couple of dun-coloured horses grazing up to my right and I figured I must be getting close to the Alpeggio Maccagno, the only habitation in the upper Valle Vogna.

I rounded a hill and came to a swampy moor. There was a small lake on the right that butted against the base of a cliff. To the left of the lake, on top of a rise, emerging from the mist, were two low stone buildings that looked like they had been thrown there by chance, the Alpeggio Maccagno. I walked around the edge of the swamp and up the bare hill towards the buildings, wading through a soup of mud and cow shit. It was a medieval scene and perhaps not by chance.

As I approached the buildings, I could hear dogs barking, their chains rattling on the paving stones. A young man with thick blond hair emerged from the upper floor of the first building. He leant over the balcony, watching me as I walked through the mud.

To my surprise, he yelled 'G'day!' in a pretty good version of an Australian accent. 'Come up here and get out of the rain.'

I climbed up the stairs towards him. He pushed the door open and stuck out his hand. 'Bruno,' he said as he ushered me in. I dipped my head and stepped into a low, dimly lit room with a small fire burning in the corner.

'Hang your stuff up over there,' he said, waving at some pegs near the door, 'and don't worry about that.' He pointed at the water pooling on the floor. 'Would you like a coffee?'

I sat at a bench at the table and looked around. Two wet pups stood shivering at the door, begging permission to come in.

He brought over two small cups of coffee. 'Do you mind?' I asked as I pulled out one of the large rolls that Sandro had prepared.

'Nah. Go for it.'

'How come your English is so good?' I asked between bites.

He laughed and explained that when he finished uni, he had backpacked and worked around Australia for twelve months. He told me that after he had returned to Italy, he had gone back to live with his family in Gattinara, a small town on the plains near Novara. There was no work around this summer so he came up here for the season. 'It's not a bad job,' he said. 'I don't mind the solitude. I like nature and staying with the animals. My boss is OK. He's a bit of a ... how do you say, *rompi scatole*?'

'Grump,' I replied.

'Yes, a bit of a grump but, you know, OK. He is away for some days. He took two pack horses and walked down the valley to deliver some cheese and to get some food and stuff.'

I looked around the room. 'How old is this place?' I asked.

He walked me over to the far wall and pointed to two inscriptions, names that had been crudely carved into the wall. 'These are the names of two *magari* who brought their herds up here a long time ago,' he said.

They read 'Sella J 1583' and 'G Sela 1762'.

'Wow,' I said with genuine surprise. 'That would make this building nearly 500 years old? Presuming the dates are for real, of course. I mean, someone could just have been bored and mucking around at some stage.'

'No, I don't think so,' he said. 'Have you seen outside the building? I think it could be older than that.'

I acknowledged he had a point. It certainly looked the part.

We went back to the table. I finished my roll and we had a second coffee.

Bruno then took me out to the *crotin*, a small stone building out the back. As he unlatched the door, we were enveloped by the damp, pungent smell of ageing cheese. On the top shelf was a row of freshly pressed wheels of white cheese, a foot across and four inches thick. The middle shelf was crowded with the mid-term wheels. The old-timers were on the lowest shelf, plump and golden, covered with a dusting of grey mould.

Back upstairs, Bruno cut me a thick slice of cheese. It was delicious. I learned later that Macagn, one of Piedmont's most celebrated cheese styles, has its origins up here. The name of the cheese is a corruption of the *alpeggio*'s own name. I learned that cheese is usually made from a combination of the morning and evening milks. Rennet, the coagulant, is stirred in and the milk is gently heated to cause the coagulation of the fatty curds from the liquid whey. The Alpeggio Maccagno is over 2000 metres above sea level, the highest cheesemaker in the Alps, and is well above the tree line. Gathering wood and transporting it up here every day was too hard, too time-consuming, so the cheese was made immediately after each milking, using the natural heat of the milk to cause the separation. This unusual technique produced a delicate cheese with a buttery aroma and a sweet subtle taste. These days Macagn is industrially produced down on the plains, the milk blended and artificially heated. I doubted very much it was as good as the cheese I had just tasted, straight out of the *crotin*.

I said goodbye to Bruno and wished him well, patted the dogs before setting out again, squelching south around the edge of the lake. It turned out that I was going in the right direction but I had taken the wrong way. I came to a big drop on the other side of the lake, a cascade of wet boulders. I didn't like the look of it but climbed down anyway. Halfway down, I slipped on a rock. The backpack lurched to one side, taking my equilibrium with it, and I found myself in a wedge, with my backpack twisted above me and my right leg folded behind me, my foot pinned to my lower back. I extricated myself from the wedge and slowly stretched my knee which, to my surprise, was undamaged. For fifteen very careful minutes I slowly worked my way down to the flats below.

It took nearly an hour to cover 2 kilometres to reach the first of several bridges I needed to cross. As I approached the bridge, I spotted a petite figure, stylishly dressed in contemporary active wear, her bright yellow pack cover standing out starkly amongst the dreary grey rocks. She was the first person I had seen walking the trail since I had left the *rifugio* that morning. I didn't feel like company but the hiker did. She stopped and waited for me.

We crossed the bridge together and chatted for the rest of the hike. I found out that Paola was forty-five and worked in a clothing factory. She was divorced and she had a five-year-old son. She had grown up in Alagna but now lived in Turin.

Paola had taken a week's holiday, staying in the lower Valle Vogna and doing day walks from there. She was on her way back from a solo walk up to the Casera Nuova Pass. She knew all about the war in the Valsesia but didn't know anything about the Allied prisoners of war escaping. She wasn't a great listener, which was OK with me, as she knew a lot about the Valle Vogna and was happy to share it.

Shortly after we crossed the bridge, the valley curved to the north-east and began to soften. It opened up, the walls becoming less abrupt, and the torrent widened and deepened. Low willows and alders clung to the rocky banks; scraggly pines ventured up the slopes. The rocky trail kept close to the river. Larches formed a prickly canopy overhead and ferns reached out to us from either side. I still had to keep my head down and watch my footing on the gnarly limestone trail, but I could also relax a bit and start to enjoy the picturesque landscape we were walking through.

At one point Paola stopped and pointed up to a tiny timber house balanced on a ridge, barely visible through the pine trees. 'People still live up there,' she said.

'Still?' I asked, incredulous. There were no roads and I

couldn't even make out a track.

'Yes,' she said. 'Not all year around though, just in the warm weather. They take their cattle up there to graze in the spring and then take them higher up in the summer when the snow has melted. They gradually bring them back down in the autumn. Vertical commuters.' She laughed. 'Cows were very important in the past. They were protein factories. If you had five or six cows, you were doing well. You could provide for your family and trade the cheese. If you had four cows, you were getting by but if you only had one or two, it was pretty tough.'

'How old are those houses?' I asked.

'I don't know,' she said, giving it some thought. 'Maybe they were first built in the 1300s or 1400s. That's when people started settling in these valleys. It was amazing what they did. This was very wild, untouched country. They had to fell the trees, clear the rocks, build terraces so they had some flat land. Till the soil. It took them generations. You should go up there. It's fantastic. There are a couple of places you can stay in, I think.' She paused. 'Shall I keep going or am I boring you?'

'Please. Carry on. It's great. I love hearing this stuff.'

'Well, that side,' she said over her shoulder as we continued down the path, pointing up to the right, 'is the south side of the valley, the *adret*. It gets the sun. It's warm in the summer and mild in the winter, so that is where they mostly built their homes and where they grew their crops and cleared their pastures.'

'So what did they grow?'

'I don't know. Potatoes, cabbages, turnips, beans, that kind of thing. A bit dreary, really. And that,' she said, pointing to the left, 'is the north-facing side, the *ubac*, so it doesn't get much sun. It's cool in summer and freezing in winter. So they left that side to the forest. But they managed it. That's where they'd get their timber, firewood. It's where they'd find mushrooms, berries and hunt game.'

We kept walking in silence for a while, but she couldn't resist.

'You know,' she said, stopping to make her point. 'The strange thing is that those people never went above the tree line. Why would you, I suppose? There was nothing there for them, just rocks and ice, maybe some animals. They were actually scared of the high mountains and the peaks. They believed dragons lived there. Right up until the late 1700s. Funny, isn't it? These days people can't get enough of the peaks. Look at Mount Everest. They are literally dying to get there. Did you know Mont Blanc has put a daily limit on the number of climbers? The new limit is 240 a day. Crazy.' She shook her head.

'Have you done any climbing?' I asked.

'Sure,' she replied, 'I grew up in Alagna, but nothing too serious.'

An hour and a half after we met, we came to a fork in the trail at a small, arched stone bridge. 'Il Ponte Napoleonico,' Paola announced, the Napoleonic Bridge. She told me that we could get to the Valle del Lys, in the Valle d'Aosta, following the path up the hill to the left. It was a tough two-hour hike from the bridge to the ridge, Colle Valdobbia. She explained that back in the day, the little trail offered a short cut into what was then France. For centuries the path had been an emigration route for many of the people of Valsesia going for seasonal work. But they weren't the only people to use what is now known as the Antica Via d'Aosta. On 20 May 1800, 400 Austrian troops were isolated in the Valle del Lys by Napoleon's army's thrust into the Valle d'Aosta. The troops escaped by climbing the Antica Via from Gressoney up to the Colle Valdobbia and then down into the Valle Vogna. A day later, 2561 French soldiers came in hot pursuit, up and over the pass. They stormed down into the Valle Vogna and then into the Valsesia, where the Austrians made a stand. The French swept them aside and carried on, re-joining their main force at Sesto Calende. This, Paola told me, by way of explaining how the bridge got its name.

Once we were over the Napoleonic Bridge, the hardest part of the day was behind us but Paola said there was still at least another hour's walking ahead of us to get to Sant'Antonio. The well-paved path wrapped around a gentle slope above the river, a pretty Alpine church peeping at us through larch trees on the crest of the hill. As we climbed up to the church, we had to stand off to the side of the track to make way for a man leading two swaying horses laden with wicker baskets, Christo-wrapped in blue tarpaulin against the rain. They were heading back up the mountain. I'm sure it was Bruno's master returning to the Alpeggio Maccagno but his stony face didn't invite conversation.

The small church was a tall building. It had a narrow façade topped with a steep gabled roof covered in grey stone tiles and a slim bell tower. Strangely, the church had turned its back to the hamlets and towns of the lower valley, facing instead the uninhabited head of the valley, from where we had arrived. I supposed this was designed to welcome the emigres returning down the Antica Via d'Aosta but it could also have been designed to protect the hamlets and villages from the evil that these travellers might bring from abroad. The church was dedicated to San Grato, a fifth-century bishop of Aosta, who was a protector against the plagues and other contagious diseases.

The pretty church was but a prelude to what lay on the other side of the ridge. Momentarily released from the steep walls of the upper valley, the river meandered in sweeping curves across gently sloping meadows before straightening up and disappearing into another gorge. There were half a dozen timber houses with slate roofs scattered across the fields, quite different to the tall stone houses of the Valle Cervo.

This gathering of houses, barely a hamlet, is called Peccia. It is the oldest settlement in the Valle Vogna, established in 1325 by Walser, German-speaking people from Valle del Lys who arrived in the Valle Vogna via the Antica Via d'Aosta. The Walser fled religious persecution in south-eastern Germany in the eighth century, moving south into the Valais, the uppermost valley of the Rhone River in western Switzerland. They were on the move again in the thirteenth century, when a brief period of global warming melted the high glaciers that had blocked access to the south. The Walser took the Teodul Pass under the Matterhorn and crossed over into what is now Italy, settling first in the Valle del Lys and then coming over the mountains and into the Valle Vogna. Until roads were put through in the late nineteenth century, the Walser stayed in the upper parts of the valleys that radiated out from Monte Rosa. They had little interest in pushing south into Italy, preferring to use the Alpine passes to the north to live and trade with their kin in the other valleys, in Switzerland and also in Germany.

Because of this, the Walser have managed to maintain their distinct identity. Their language, Titsch, an archaic form of German, is still widely spoken. The most obvious manifestation of their difference, however, is their unique style of architecture: stone and wood houses, a cunning response to a harsh climate. The classic Walser house is a large structure, usually three levels. Stone on the ground floor for animals, workspaces and the hearth; timber on the top for the storage of winter fodder, usually hay. Sandwiched between the two, the sleeping areas, snug between the warmth below and insulation above. It is covered by a vast, overhanging roof covered in split stone tiles, supported at the edges by interlocking wooden piers that are connected obliquely to the central structure, like the struts on a biplane's wings.

There wasn't much movement when Paola and I walked through the hamlet, only a woman who waved at us from a geranium-covered verandah. On the other side of the hamlet, we came to a parking area. The path became an unsealed road. We carried on along this road as it wound through forest above the river, hoping that Sant'Antonio would appear around every corner.

Finally, it did. A jumble of Walser houses tumbling down the hill to another small church with a tall belltower, Sant'Antonio. Opposite this, across the road was a small building overlooking the river, the Rifugio Valle Vogna. It had taken seven-and-a-half hours of steady hiking and I was very pleased to get there.

Paola didn't have time for a drink as she was staying at a classier place a couple of kilometres downhill and was keen to get there before dark. She had been great company, helping to take the sting out of a challenging hike. We said our farewells and I unloaded my backpack, stretched my shoulders, then ducked through a low doorway into a cosy bar. The barkeeper was expecting me, as Sandro from the Rifugio Rivetti had called through to let him know I was on my way.

He was a tall, sad-looking man with salt-and-pepper hair and a wall eye. He shook my hand and poured me a litre of beer in a very large glass stein, which I carried back outside. I sat on a stone bench by the entrance to the church, unlaced my boots and leant back against the wall, enjoying the view.

After a couple of minutes, Carl Carrigan and his mates came shuffling back into my consciousness. I had been concentrating too much on negotiating my own way down through the rocky terrain to give them much thought. They would have come down the same paths that I had walked and maybe even rested on the same stone bench I was sitting on. Lloyd Ledingham, one of the group, mentioned Sant'Antonio but Carl didn't name it. Carl didn't dwell on the details of this section of their escape. It had taken them three days to cross the mountains from Piedicavallo to Sant'Antonio and they hadn't eaten anything in that time. They dropped down into the valley, ready to beg, borrow or steal food.

It had taken me two days to get from the Valle Cervo to Sant'Antonio. Unlike the men, I was walking at the end of a mild summer. I had all the equipment I needed. I had lodgings along the way and I was well fed. I carried a good map and the trails I followed were well marked; and yet, my feet were sore, I had made mistakes and had almost badly injured myself. It had been a challenge, pushing me hard in parts. Once more, it was difficult to comprehend what the men had faced: poor clothes, no food, behind enemy lines, with no directions home.

Beer finished, I picked up my pack and returned inside. Without much conversation, my host directed me up a rickety flight of stairs past a smelly bathroom on the landing halfway up. At the top were two dormitories. Mine was the one on the right. I drew the curtain aside and looked into a small room filled with Ikea beds, a double bunk near the entrance and three narrow single beds pushed under the sloping roof of the ceiling. Two beds were already taken. I claimed the single nearest the door, took my clean clothes and the microfibre towel out of my pack and flopped down to the tiny bathroom in my thongs. No laundry tonight.

Revived by the hot shower, I followed the aromas downstairs to the dining room, a small room next to the bar with half a dozen cubicles. I slipped into one with a couple, who turned out to be Swiss. The barkeeper was also the waiter. He brought over a short but interesting menu. I ordered a half-litre of red wine, feeling I'd earnt it, and ordered my meal, comparing hiking notes with the Swissies as I waited for the food to arrive. The first dish was agnolotti, a small local version of ravioli, knotted rather than pinched, which were stuffed with veal and served in a broth. Delicious. The rabbit stew that followed was exceptional: deboned pieces slow-cooked in white wine with diced yellow bell-peppers, accompanied by tossed spinach and roasted potatoes. We all finished with a generous serve of the inevitable *bunet* and a fiery glass of grappa.

Above: At the Rifugio Rivetti looking down towards the Valle Cervo.

Below: San Grato, on the edge of the village of Peccia, Valle Vogna.

Above: San Michele, the parish church of Alagna.

Below: A Walser house in the upper Valsesia with the snow-capped Monte Rosa in the background.

CHAPTER 6

Sant'Antonio to Rifugio Pastore
11 kilometres, 628-metre ascent, 3 hours

The bed was too short and poorly sprung but I slept well nonetheless, waking up in the half-light when the earliest risers started banging around and talking loudly. I had a short walk ahead of me so I rolled over and played possum. Breakfast was generous: yoghurt, fresh fruit, a basket of bread, wedges of cheese, freshly sliced prosciutto and a large pot of coffee. I didn't slip anything into my pocket this time – I was planning on lunch in Alagna.

After I'd finished, I had a chat with the barkeeper. He was hard to read but it seemed that he was interested, possibly fascinated, by my story. He wandered out from behind the bar, slowly nodding his head and muttering with surprise,

'*Ma pensa te? Pensa te?*' How about that?

'I was born and raised in Sant'Antonio,' he explained, one elbow on the bar. 'My grandmother used to tell me stories about Allied escapees coming down the valley. They were hungry and scared and had the arse out of their pants. She used to help them. You know, give them some food, maybe let them sleep in the barn. She never mentioned Australians. For her they are all *inglesi*, English. But,' he added, 'you never know, maybe your uncle …'

I had the same thought. 'Your grandmother must have been very brave,' I said.

'Well,' he leant against the bar, 'not necessarily. You see, the valley was full of women and the Germans behaved themselves well in these parts. My grandmother said it was the partisans who were the problem around here. Blowing things up, stealing things, shooting people.'

I explained the route that Carl and his friends had taken.

The barkeeper nodded. 'They were smart. The most obvious route would have been to go over the mountains into the Valle del Lys, and then up the Valle d'Aosta and head for the Gran San Bernardo Pass. But that would have been heavily patrolled and dangerous. No one would have expected them to come down the Valle Vogna. *Sono stati bravi. Davero bravi.*' Or lucky, as the case may be.

When his wife joined us, he got me to roll out the story once more. She was very interested as well, quite animated.

When I had finished, she smiled and thanked me for the story, as if it were a gift.

It was a beautiful day. The rain had stopped, the clouds had gone, the sun was shining and there was a clear blue sky above me. I headed down the road, the forested slopes of the Valle Vogna rising above me on either side. After 3 kilometres of slapping along the asphalt, a small, faded sign directed me down a path to the right: Via Antica d'Aosta. It was a beautiful remnant of the old trail, a flat path paved with river stones that led steeply downhill through beech forest. It was a short cut that avoided more hairpin bends on the road and brought me quickly down to the outer buildings of Riva Valdobbia.

This small tidy town sits on a flat morainic terrace, a platform of rubble disgorged by the Vogna glacier as it flows into the far larger glacier in the Valsesia. The town looks over the Sesia River to the treeless northern wall of the valley. As I wound my way down narrow lanes between tall stone apartment blocks and restored Walser houses surrounded by carefully tended gardens, I caught glimpses of Monte Rosa, which loomed large at the head of the valley on my left.

I arrived at the main square of Riva, Piazza Quattro Novembre, and decided to have a cappuccino at Da Mario, a small bar on the corner that had tables in the square. I sipped my cappuccino and caught up on the *Gazzetta dello Sport*, admiring the alarming fresco of the Last Judgement that covered the façade of the church of St Michele on my left. I felt like I was on holiday, a feeling Carl and his mates might have shared when they finally arrived in Riva. They were back in friendly country.

Like the Valle Cervo, which the group left three days earlier, the Valsesia was a stronghold of the resistance, only an even greater one. It is in the heart of the Cusiane Alps, a 6500-hectare range of inaccessible mountains that have been carved and shaped by glaciers. The Valsesia is a sinuous valley that snakes through these mountains. It is 60 kilometres long, starting at Prato Sesia at the entrance to the valley and finishing at Alagna at the end.

Several sizable towns stretch along the lower valley floor but there is nothing much between Varallo and Alagna, the last 35 kilometres, just a few stone hamlets, squeezed between the high, narrow walls of the valley and the banks of the Sesia River.

The Fascist regime was never accepted in these remote places. The farmers were always independent. The miners of the upper valley and the men and women who worked in the textile, machine and paper factories in the lower valley were unionised and hardened by a tradition of strikes, many of them card-carrying members of the Communist Party. The steep, heavily forested walls of the valley provided shelter and refuge for the rebels.

Immediately after the armistice, the Committee of the Resistance of the Valsesia was created, nominating Cino Moscatelli, a long-time operative of the Italian Communist Party, as the valley's military commander. He was an intelligent and audacious leader who would become a legendary figure, eventually leading the victorious partisan forces into Piazza Duomo in Milan on 26 April 1945. At this early stage, Moscatelli had the responsibility of coordinating the disparate partisan groups that were coalescing in the valley, around one hundred people at the beginning, divided into three groups.

The history of the war in the Valsesia is intertwined with the story of another extraordinary ex-alumni of Campo 106: Sapper Jens Francis Jocumsen, a larger-than-life figure from Maryborough on the central Queensland coast. He was best known as Frank Jocumsen, but he had other nicknames: Butch, Frank l'Australiano, Franck and French.

There are almost as many myths about Jocumsen as there are about Moscatelli. Frank was not an Australian boxing champion, although he could throw a good punch. He was not awarded the Medaglia d'Oro, Italy's highest military decoration. Nor was he granted freedom of the city of Varallo by the Italian president, and he was definitely not the military commander of the Garibaldi Brigade in the Valsesia, as he told a reporter on his arrival back in Australia in 1945. He was, however, a very good soldier – highly respected by Cino Moscatelli, who always kept Frank close and mentioned him many times in his post-war account of the resistance in the Valsesia called 'Il Monte Rosa e Sceso a Milano (Monte Rosa descends to Milan)'.

Frank was born in 1912. Before the war he was a butcher, like his father, hence his first nickname. He enlisted in the AIF in May 1940. Like Carl Carrigan, he left for the Middle East on the *Orion* in November 1940. Like Carl, he was taken prisoner in North Africa, did time in Grupignano and then Campo 106 in Vercelli. Unlike Carl, on release in September, he headed north. In an interview recorded when he returned to Varallo in 1979, in a slow, deep voice, Frank said:

> I heard that it was safer to go north to the town of Varallo, where there was some resistance and there was someone who could guide us to Switzerland. In Vercelli, I met a local student who put me in touch with his father. The father gave me civilian clothes and then accompanied me by train to Varallo. From here, I was taken into the mountains by Leo [likely Leo Colombo, one of the original members of the band and a popular Alpine guide] and that's where I met the partisans.

Frank would have been a great asset for the inexperienced rebels. His Italian companions described him as a big, confident man, courageous and generous. Moscatelli recognised his qualities and quickly gave him significant responsibilities, starting with guiding a group of POWs over the mountains to Switzerland and then incorporating him into the fighting, mainly as a machine-gunner. Frank spent over a year fighting with the partisans, including being involved in the short-lived liberation of the valley in June 1944.

On 1 July of that year, after a clandestine visit to John McCaffery, British Military Attache and SOE Station Officer in Berne, Jocumsen was made the British Liaison Officer with the partisans north of Novara. McCaffery later said that Frank was something of a legend and that his reputation had preceded him long before they met. Frank was provided with identity papers and given the temporary rank of captain. He was also outfitted, which included a slouch hat that he wore throughout the rest of the campaign, as well as a Thompson machine gun, a very effective weapon, which his partisan companions had only seen in the movies.

In December 1944, Frank was ordered back to Switzerland and did not return to the Valsesia again until 1979 when Cino Moscatelli, who by then was a Communist Party member of the Italian government, invited him to return to Varallo, where the mayor gave him the honorary keys to the town. Unlike his younger colleague in Milan, John Peck, Frank never received any official recognition for his remarkable service in the mountains of northern Italy. There were rumours of bad behaviour (one example being that Frank was supposed to have decked two American military police who were harassing him during a visit to Rome), but the most likely theory is that Frank was too close to Cino Moscatelli, an unacceptable association in Robert Menzies' fervently anti-Communist Australia in the 1950s.

I like to think my Uncle John might have joined the partisans too rather than continuing on to the Swiss border. It is, of course, impossible to say. Both John and Frank were Queenslanders, after all, but it took a very game person to throw in their lot with one of these loose rebel groups at this early stage. They would have been rather motley crews, little more than young, leaderless deserters who had been the POWs' enemies less than two weeks earlier.

It is not known how many Allied soldiers joined the Garibaldi Brigades, but it has been estimated that thirteen died fighting with the partisans in these valleys, Brits and Anzacs included. Moscatelli wrote that two other Allied soldiers joined at the same time as Frank: David, an Englishman; and Pat, *'un piccolo soldato irlandese'*, a little Irish soldier. By the end of 1943, approximately twenty more Allied soldiers had joined the force, but Moscatelli complained that on the first serious contact with German soldiers in mid-January, most of these men threw down their arms and headed for Switzerland.

Frank Jocumsen would have barely met his new partisan chums above Varallo when Carl and his mates arrived in the upper Valsesia in late September 1943. As the bedraggled men approached the houses of Riva Valdobbia, excited school children surrounded them and led them to the main square. Here they were seated, and bowls of macaroni and potatoes were brought to them, the little that the villagers could spare. They were also brought bottles of *vino*, a rough homebrew that the soldiers only drank out of politeness, reluctant to offend the generosity of their hosts.

By the time they left Riva, Carl and his friends were in good spirits. They didn't bother going bush but walked straight up the main road to Alagna, 3 kilometres away at the head of the valley. When they heard a vehicle coming up the valley behind them, they didn't even take the trouble to run for cover. Fortunately, it was a road maintenance crew who stopped and gave the weary soldiers a lift into town. The crew then took them to a bar, where they were welcomed by the patrons and shouted drinks and food until the end of the evening.

Sadly, I wasn't so lucky. I had to walk all the way along the road to Alagna and I also had to pay for my own drinks once I got there. Alagna is the largest town in the upper valley. It has 700 inhabitants. It is completely surrounded by mountains. The most dramatic of these was straight in front of me as I walked up the road: her majesty, Monte Rosa. Not a single summit like Mont Blanc or the Matterhorn, Monte Rosa is a massif, a rounded snow-covered ridge that has twenty-two separate peaks over 4000 metres high. The closest to the Valsesia is Punta Gniffetti, named after the parish priest who was the first to climb it, on 9 August 1842. Monte Rosa must have been a sobering sight for the soldiers. The mountain forms the border between Italy and Switzerland. Freedom was in sight, but Europe's second-highest mountain, with its snow and glaciers, stood between them. So near and yet so far.

Alagna was settled after Peccia. This time the Walser had walked directly from the Valais in Switzerland a hundred years later, crossing the Passo del Turlo from Macugnaga, the same route I would be taking but in reverse. After Padre Gnifetti's achievement in 1842, Alagna became a popular mountaineering destination. It has the third-oldest Alpine guide association in the mountains, after Chamonix and Courmayeur. In the 1970s Alagna became a popular ski resort, particularly with 'free-skiers' who still enjoy its wilder, untouched runs.

Today Alagna has a dual personality, international ski-bums rubbing shoulders with the well-heeled of Milan and Turin. Once you get past the mess of roads and low-rise apartment blocks on the outskirts of town, the centre is very attractive, a mix of impeccably restored Walser houses, elegant fin-de-siècle palazzi and high-end stores, all inter-connected by paved footways and neat gardens. In the middle proudly stands the parish church of San Michele with its tall, stone belltower forming a late-Gothic roundabout.

To get to the main square I had to squeeze through the traffic and around the bulging apse of the church. On the other side, between the church's entrance and the Albergo Monterosa, was a very pleasant, paved piazza shaded by a large pine tree. In front of the square, on the right of the church, was the *campo santo*, the cemetery, the tops of the mausoleums of the richer families peering over the stone wall that enclosed it. On the right side of the cemetery, on a wall farthest from the church, was a large marble plaque with a row of seventeen small iron crosses. They mark the place where seventeen rebels, nine partisans and eight ex-Carabinieri were executed in a reprisal killing by the Fascists on 14 July 1944 after the collapse of the uprising in the Valsesia.

On the other side of the piazza, under the arcade of the Albergo Monterosa, is the Café delle Guide, the oldest bar in town. It was here that I imagined Carl and his friends enjoyed the hospitality of the locals, finally in the company of friends, safe, at least for the moment. It was a smart place when I was there, its barrel ceiling discreetly illuminated by neon lights, soft music playing and a hip barista waiting for me as I walked in. Sepia photos on the walls showed that it was very different in days past when mountain guides with handlebar moustaches, dressed in battered trilby hats and patched corduroy suits, waited patiently outside for work. I ordered a panino and a glass of mineral water and sat at a table under the shade of the old pine tree.

While the soldiers were carousing at the bar, they were told how to get to Switzerland. It was impossible to go over the top of Monte Rosa, so they would have to follow a path that skirted around to the east side of the mountain. The path climbed up to the Passo del Turlo and then down the other side, through the Valle Quarazza to Macugnaga, a town in the Valle Anzasca. They would be almost there. The Swiss border was on the ridge on the northern side of Valle Anzasca. With the early winter of 1943, there was already snow on the pass but that, they were told, wouldn't present a problem: it was a long, hard climb but the path was good. People had been using it for centuries. Turlo, in fact, is a Walser name. It means 'the little door', a door that led the Walser to a new life and would lead the POWs to freedom.

At the end of their night of revelry at the bar in Alagna, one of Carl's drinking companions offered to take the soldiers further into the mountains. He had some cows up there that had to be brought down to avoid the coming weather. The soldiers could spend the night in his *rustico*, he said. It was on the way to the pass.

They followed the man out of town, going north towards the end of the valley. The POWs were exhausted, and the climb was relentless. It was particularly difficult for Lloyd, who was suffering a groin injury. At one point the group stopped to rest and they asked their companion how far they had still to go. He pointed out a distant waterfall and told them it was beyond that. Their hearts sank further. They pressed on, of course, and eventually came to a small stone house with a slate roof in a clearing. '*Casa mia*,' the man announced. He ushered them in. They built a small fire, curled up under blankets on the floor and went to sleep.

I followed the same route out of town as the soldiers did. It was the only way: a narrow road to the north that ran beside the river. I passed the houses of Pedemonte, the last settlement in the valley, and then a disused manganese mine, a ruin swallowed up by brambles, once the pride of the town. After passing a small chapel, as the road curved, I came to a footbridge that crossed the river. I took this, happy to leave the road. On the other side, I picked up a beautiful stone path that dipped and climbed through dappled forest.

An hour after leaving Alagna, another bridge took me back over the river to the road. I crossed it and took a smaller trail on the left that climbed steeply through pine and chestnut forests. The valley narrowed and the sides started closing in around me. I passed a waterfall and thought of the soldiers. After thirty minutes' climbing, the path levelled out and I left the forest. A small, impeccably restored Walser house, with the standard rows of geraniums running along the wooden verandah, smiled down at me. I had arrived at the Rifugio Pastore, on the pastures of the Alpe Pile, at the head of the Valsesia.

The *rifugio* was originally a collection of small stone houses that the shepherds had used in the summer. It is possible the soldiers spent the night in one of these houses. The abandoned hamlet had been restored in the 1970s, converted into the *rifugio*. The smaller houses were turned into dormitories, each room with three or four bunk beds. They also added a large ablutions block. The largest house was converted into a common area. It had the reception, a bar and a restaurant as well as a wide terrace out the back that looked straight up at the southern face of Monte Rosa.

I followed the moss-covered stairs around the first house, under the overhanging eves of the dormitory houses to the reception. I left my pack outside. A cheerful young woman greeted me from behind the bar. No need for passports or documentation here, just a name and how many nights I intended to stay. I ordered a large beer and a bag of crisps and walked out onto the terrace. I sat down at a bench and looked around me.

A wide, grassy field rolled out in front of me, divided by a paved path. Behind this, forests converged from either side of the canyon. Beyond the forests, the belly of the enormous mountain closed the valley. I spread my map out on the bench in front of me. I identified three peaks that had broken through the cloud cover: Vincent Pyramid on the left; Punta Parrot, lower in the middle; and Punta Gnifetti, the highest, on the right, 3000 metres above where I was sitting. The two grey arms of a glacier, Ghiacciaio delle Piode, split around a wall of stone, retreating towards the crest of the mountain, the last remnant of the ancient glacier that had carved out the Valsesia. Icy water gushed from the end of each arm feeding a multitude of streams that cascade over cliffs at the base, the source of the Sesia River.

One of the staff came out onto the terrace to collect empty glasses. I asked her where the Passo del Turlo was. She turned and pointed up into the forest on her right. '*Quella direzione.*'

'Is there any snow up there?' I asked.

'*Non lo so. Potrebbe esserci.*' She didn't know about the snow but there could be some up there, which wasn't very encouraging. Would I like another beer?

'*Sì grazie. Ma solo una piccola, per favore.*'

I sat out on the terrace, sipped my beer and watched the shadows creep up the face of the mountain. I was worried about the hike tomorrow and had been for most of the week. On paper it was the most daunting leg: a very long haul with a big, steep climb at the beginning. I was also worried about walking through snow and ice. The day before, Paola had shown me photos on her phone of snowdrifts she had negotiated a few days earlier. I imagined that the rain of the days before would have brought snow to the higher parts. The weather predictions for the next day were good for the morning but there was a change coming through in the afternoon, the chance of rain in the valleys and snow on the mountains. The hiking of the previous days was also starting to take its toll. I had blisters on both heels, an ache in the arch of my right foot and a strain in my right calf; but, despite my concerns, I was looking forward to the challenge.

~

I discovered my passion for hiking by accident. I had kind of enjoyed bushwalking and camping when I was a kid growing up in Canberra, but I had never truly embraced it. My earliest experiences involved marching in single file through the tinder-dry sclerophyll bush of the Monaro, avoiding bull ants and snakes, while Colonel and Mrs

Langtry led us to cleared camping areas where we would pitch our canvas tents under the sagging limbs of ageing gum trees and sing 'Kumbaya', sitting around a blazing fire, toasting marshmallows on the end of a long stick.

As I got older, bushwalking began to represent a kind of freedom, an escape. With a group of school friends, I'd be driven out of Canberra by a parent and dropped off at a not-too-distant waterway, perhaps the Cotter Dam or the banks of the Murrumbidgee River. Laden with trout-fishing gear, backpacks, tents, cans of baked beans, crushed bags of sliced white bread and sleeping bags filled with cigarettes and flasks of vodka, we would be waved off and then hike up the river as far as necessary to guarantee our privacy but no further. We would then spend unsupervised weekends in teenage revelry, untangling fishing line from low-hanging branches, smoking cigarettes and eating burnt jaffles.

Then, when I was in my mid-twenties and living in Milan, I discovered the real joy of hiking. It was a revelation. It was 1983 and I was teaching English to adults at a dubious language school in the centre of Milan. Two of my colleagues, Ray and Dale, invited me to join them on a bike ride up to Lake Como for the weekend. I had barely left the city since arriving and agreed on the spot. They fixed me up with a rattly, second-hand bike that only had one gear, but I was young and keen.

We rode out of the city to the north, following busy freeways and narrow lakeside lanes to Menaggio, halfway up the eastern shore of the lake. At the end of an 80-kilometre ride, we chained our bikes to a fence near a carpark, slung our packs on our backs and walked up a steep, winding road to the village of Breglia. From here, we climbed for an hour, following slippery stone mule trails through damp forest to the Rifugio Menaggio, a mountain lodge tucked under the towering cliffs of Monte Grona.

After cold showers, we had beers on the terrace enjoying breathtaking views over the lake. We had our dinner inside: steaming polenta, beef stew and carafes of rough red wine, eaten at a crowded communal table in a refectory full of young Italians. We slept on rickety bunk beds in a cramped dormitory, fuggy with damp clothes and old boots.

After a breakfast of stale biscuits dunked in bowls of hot coffee, we climbed more stone paths through misty forests, over to the neighbouring valley, arriving at a tiny, neglected hamlet that seemed to have been swallowed up by the trees. We thought it was abandoned until an old man dressed in a patched tweed coat came out of a creaking wooden door and greeted us. We tried to converse but didn't get anywhere.

As we were leaving, following our steps back to the *rifugio*, I paused and turned around. The old man was still watching us with his watery eyes; I imagined he didn't get many visitors. I waved and he raised his hand slowly in reply and then turned and disappeared into his home. I looked at the boarded windows and decaying houses. We were only two hours away from the great metropolis and yet here I stood in this ancient settlement that had been there for who knows how long. There were no cars, no phones, a two-hour descent down a winding path to the nearest shop for provisions, and yet there were people still living here – well, one person at least. I felt like I had stepped back in time.

The following spring, in 1984, I caught a train south to Corniglia with the same friends. We crossed the cold, foggy plains of Lombardy to the Ligurian coast, where we were greeted by sunshine, palm trees and warm breezes. Cristina, the secretary at our school, had rung ahead and booked us into an apartment. It was the only accommodation in the sleepy village of Corniglia, the middle village of the Cinque Terre – a string of five fishing villages dug into the cliffs of the Apennine mountains between Genova and La Spezia. The apartment was owned by Signora Sporra, a short, broad and ebullient lady with tight dark hair and a gapped smile. She lived in a large house near the railway station and met us on the platform as our train pulled in. We followed her up endless zigzagging stairs to the village, which stretched along a narrow ridge and finished at a walled belvedere that looked out over the sea.

Corniglia had a small *alimentare*, or general store, called Bar Matteo and a *cantina* at the entrance to the village where the local white wine could be bought by the litre, and that was it. Fortunately, we had brought our own provisions. The apartment had a good kitchen, so we spent the weekend cooking, eating, drinking and exploring the trails that radiated out from the village.

On the first walk, we began with a steep climb up stone stairs through vineyards. After an hour we reached the top, where we had to stop to catch our breath. We tacked east through more vineyards, with wide views out across the sparkling sea, and then back down endless jarring stairs to the neighbouring village of Manarola. We followed another path around the headland to the village of Riomaggiore. It was barely a mule trail and we had to scramble over two landslips. We caught the train back to Corniglia.

On another, we followed a looping coastal walk through forests and vineyards to Vernazza, a village tucked into a steepling bay. It was the most beautiful place I had ever seen. Along the way, we passed a string of donkeys laden with building materials and met two boys grubbing in the scrub beside the trails, looking for wild asparagus. They gave us a handful of the thin, whippy shoots for dinner.

Before we left Corniglia on Sunday afternoon, we stopped in at the *cantina* for takeaways. The old man sitting at the entrance raised himself painfully from his stone bench, shook our hands and motioned for us to follow him inside the cave. Up the back, in the shadows, was a row of three large wooden barrels. He picked up a bucket, placed it under the biggest barrel and turned the spigot. Sparkling white wine splashed into the bucket. He closed the spigot, dipped a tin cup into the golden liquid and then passed it to us to taste. It was delicious: light, fruity, fresh. He retrieved two empty 2-litre plastic bottles from a shopping bag hanging on the wall and filled them to the brim, screwing the caps on nice and tight. We gave him a handful of lire, shoved the bottles into our bags, shook his hand again and headed down the stairs to the train station.

Perhaps it was the train trip, or the smog and the gloomy wet streets of Milan but, whatever the cause, by the time we pulled the bottles out at dinner, the wine had lost its sparkle. The magic was gone, and it had become a sorry memory of the elixir we had enjoyed on the coast.

All the same, I was converted to hiking, Italian-style. The weather was warming, and I began to get away on the weekends as often as I could. At first, I mostly walked trails into the mountains around Lake Como but, if I had some extra time, I would get a train back down to Liguria and follow the stone paths along the coast. Walking by myself was an adventure: making all the decisions, getting lost, finding my way out again. I was alone with my thoughts, alive to everything around me.

It was getting cold on the terrace. The last rays of the sun were glowing pink on the snow on the top of Monte Rosa. I finished my drink and took my pack over to my quarters on the other side of the courtyard. I climbed up wooden stairs, sat on a bench on the verandah, took off my boots and then gently peeled off my socks, trying not to remove the gummy band-aids that were protecting my blistered heels. I padded down a small corridor and into a long dormitory, much larger than the one I had slept in the previous night.

At the sight of me, a short, middle-aged Italian man sprang up from his bed at the far end of the room and walked over to welcome me as if he had been expecting me. He introduced himself as Stefano and told me he was from Genova. He was very pleased to meet me and more so when he learned that I was Australian. He immediately switched languages to speak in pretty good English.

'Ah, Australia! It's my dream. I hope you don't mind if I practise my English. I haven't had the opportunity to use it much since I worked in Scandinavia.'

Once I'd showered, together we went back down to the restaurant and had another drink on the terrace, and then escaped the cold for the warmth of the dining room and our evening meal.

There were half a dozen other people staying at the *rifugio*. Once we were all seated at our tables, dinner started. We were brought a carafe of water and a carafe of red wine, a basket of stale buns and a wooden platter of cheeses and roughly sliced salamis and hams. Once this was cleared, there was a short pause before they brought out a copper saucepan filled with a thick rice and potato soup, with a ladle submerged. It was a bland but heart-warming brew, pepped up with a grating of sharp pecorino cheese. This was followed by a platter of handmade short pasta cooked in a pine mushroom sauce and topped with a dollop of fresh ricotta.

In the lull between courses, we called for a second carafe of red. Stefano was a nervous, energetic person who liked a chat.

'I love the mountains,' he said. 'Genova is OK, but I love to hike. I prefer to hike on my own. Don't get me wrong, I'm not antisocial. I'm not a weirdo. I just like the peace and quiet.'

This, I thought, was a bit ironic, given his propensity to chatter, but there you go. I said that I, too, enjoyed walking on my own and then I told him about my trek. He wasn't that interested.

'I'm doing the Tour de Monte Rosa, TMR. Do you know it?' he asked.

'I do know it. We are actually on it,' I pointed out.

Where the Grande Traversata delle Alpi, GTA, that had got me from Oropa to here, is more or less a straight line from the mountains to the sea, TMR is circular, more or less, and much shorter. A 164-kilometre loop around Monte Rosa, passing through Swiss and Italian territory. The two trails briefly converge at the head of the Valsesia, sharing a short stretch of trail as you walk north out of Alagna. I had left the GTA and joined the TMR when I had crossed the river and climbed up the stairs to Rifugio Pastore.

'I've done the TMR twice before,' Stefano said. 'So this is my third time. It usually takes nine or ten days but I'm going to do it in six.'

He told me that the leg I was doing the next day was the most challenging of the whole circuit, which didn't reassure me. He had done it that day, in reverse, from Macugnaga to Rifugio Pastore and, of course, he had done it in a lot less than the regulation time. I asked him about the conditions.

'Plenty of snow around,' he said, 'but not too much on the track. It shouldn't be a problem, as long as it doesn't snow tonight.'

The main course, as if we needed it, was a platter of chunked roasted chicken, not your supermarket version but the home-grown ones, with dark meat, thick bones with marrow, small feathers still protruding from the dimpled yellow skin. It was served with fresh green beans, chopped cherry tomatoes and lashings of rich gravy. There was a side dish of roasted zucchini strips.

'Have you ever been to the Rifugio Regina Margherita?' I asked. 'That, Stefano, is my dream.'

'Yes, I have. I have been there several times,' he replied.

Of course he had. Nonetheless, I was impressed. The *rifugio* is the highest building in Europe, sitting on the top of Punta Gnifetti, 4554 metres above sea level. It was named after the first queen of Italy, who hiked up here in 1893, with assistance from her entourage, to inaugurate the *rifugio*. It has been rebuilt several times since then. The latest version is a sleek steel building strapped to the edge of a long cliff by cables. On a clear day, it is visible from Alagna.

'How do you get there?' I asked.

'Well, you can go up from the Swiss side or from the Italian side,' he replied. 'I've always done it from the Italian side, from Rifugio Gnifetti, which takes a big day from Alagna, or you can take the cable-car part of the way, but that would be cheating. From Gnifetti, you climb up the Lys Glacier. It takes around five hours. You could do it on your own, but that would be very inadvisable. You have to cross ice and glaciers, so you really need a guide. You can't muck around,' he added, leaning forward. 'Just a couple of days ago, three *Alpinisti* died on the other side of the mountain. They were Swiss, lots of experience. They were crossing an ice bridge that suddenly collapsed. They were tied together. Down they went. One, two, three. Eight hundred metres.' He sat back for effect. 'There were five other guys in the team. They were unhurt. Nothing they could do. Just had to stand there and watch. *Mamamia ...*'

Dessert arrived and we changed the subject. It was an extraordinary composition of sliced fruit and sponge cake piled onto a share platter and topped with whipped cream and a generous drizzle of strawberry sauce.

Once we were done, Stefano wiped his lips with his napkin and pushed his chair back, pointing out that the food was better here than at the Rifugio Regina Margherita.

'Apart from anything else,' he said, 'the pasta never cooks properly up there because the water can't boil at such an altitude.'

We finished our meal with a coffee and a shot of their grappa and then headed to bed. We were the last to leave but we still managed an early night.

Despite Stefano's bravado, I was still worried, actually a bit scared, about the next day's hike. It was the last and the hardest and there was the prospect of snow. I had been pushed to my limits climbing up to the Rifugio Rivetti and I had been lucky not to have been seriously injured coming down the Valle Vogna the next day.

I closed my eyes and hoped for good weather.

The start of the walk to the Passo del Turlo
along the 'strada militare'.

Above: Approaching the Passo del Turlo on the 'strada militare'.

Below: Leaving the Passo del Turlo on the 'strada militare'
into the Valle Quarazza.

CHAPTER 7

Rifugio Pastore to Macugnaga
22 kilometres, 1250-metre ascent, 8 hours

Stefano woke me up early, of course, all bright eyes and bushy tail. I waved across the room and pulled the pillow over my head, taking time to compose myself. I had slept poorly, bad dreams and frequent trips out to pee under the stars – the result of anxiety, the discomfort of my ankles and probably too much beer.

People milled around the concourse in the half light, speaking in low voices, adjusting their backpacks. Inside, in the warmth and light, I joined Stefano for a big breakfast: a mug of coffee, fresh fruit and yoghurt, cold cuts and cheeses. I paid my bill, picked up the packed lunch I'd ordered the night before and thanked the staff. I filled up my CamelBak from a small fountain outside that eternally bubbled freezing water. I swung on my pack, bouncing on my toes, pulling the straps tight to get the balance right. Once again, I was the only person going north.

~~~

The soldiers didn't have as gentle a start as I had on their climb to the Passo del Turlo. They were woken up by the wife of their host, who had turned up earlier than expected. She was not pleased at all by what she found: a group of four hungover escaped POWs sleeping in her hut. They must have been quite a sight, too. Half-starved, they had been on the run for ten days, sleeping rough most nights in the bitter cold of the early winter. They were wearing the same clothes they had on when they left Biella. It was hard to tell whether she was just plain angry at the carousing or fearful of the consequences of having four fugitives in her home, or both. Either way, she was furious and ordered them on their way immediately.

The chastised husband didn't even have time to give them directions. He just pointed up the hill. Fortunately for Carl and his friends, there was only one trail up to the pass: a stone path that wound up through larch forest. It was the same path that I would be walking.

~~~

Stefano came over and seized my hand between both of his and shook it vigorously. He slapped me on the back. 'You'll be fine. No problems.'

With that, I adjusted the straps again, fiddled with the nozzle of the CamelBak and started walking along the path towards Monte Rosa.

The weather was perfect, a crisp bite in the air. It hadn't rained overnight so I was optimistic. The mountain was hidden behind a wall of clouds with smudges of light blue above the ridge promising a clearer morning.

At the end of the field, a well-made stone path curved down to the right and crossed a roofed, wooden bridge, suspended above a gorge, with the headwaters of the Sesia River crashing far below. The path curved around to the left and began to climb steadily through a forest of young fir trees, the decomposed needles softening my steps. I was excited to be on my way; the promising weather report had blown away my doubts: cloudy for the climb and then clearing when I reached the top.

I was breathing heavily. My knees and hamstrings were tight. I feared it was going to be a long day. Rather than slowing down, I pushed harder, head down, eyes on the path. After fifteen minutes, the fir trees gave way to silver birches and skinny larches. The path levelled and I caught glimpses down over the Alpe Pile and the Rifugio Pastore into the Valsesia.

I paused to enjoy the view. As always, I was surprised to see how far I had already climbed in such a short time. I guessed that I had gained around 400 metres after leaving the *rifugio* an hour earlier. The aches had gone and my breathing had calmed down, still heavy but more consistent. I felt good. I spun around, the backpack tugging me off balance, and stared up at the towering mountains that surrounded me. I recognised the forked Piode Glacier and the pointed Vincent Pyramid. To the left of this, ragged black cliffs led up to Punta Indren.

I turned back. The Valsesia had opened up in front of me, a long deep, dark valley, the steep sides rising almost 1000 metres above the river. Alagna was barely visible, a jumble of houses in the haze, but I thought I could make out the entrance to the Valle Vogna, down the valley to the right. On my left was the northern ridge-line of the valley and the Vallone Pilglimo, a scalloped amphitheatre of glacial detritus, which was topped by the peaks of Corno Rima and Corno Mud. The sun had risen above the northern crests and was trying to break through the clouds.

As I continued up the hill, I felt a sense of happiness, elation. This was what I was made for, I thought. I don't walk to find answers or consolation. My motivation is simple: I love the choreography of a long-distance walk, the satisfaction of rhythmic movement, of finding my way through unfamiliar terrain and of arriving in a place that

I have never seen before. I was born with two left feet, so hiking is my dancing.

The path contoured around a hill, leaving the trees behind, and climbed up into open land. The steep slopes were covered in thick grasses shot with yellow and purple flowers. The path weaved in and out of gullies. I crossed a wide stream, stepping carefully on slippery stones. As I rounded a corner, two indifferent donkeys with thick leather collars came ambling down the hill towards me. I stood aside and let them pass, encouraging the last one to pause so I could rub its forehead with my knuckles and scratch its long flat neck. It continued down the hill to catch up with its mate, disappearing around a corner, its thin tail lazily flicking its grey flanks.

Further up around the hill I came to a small stone house on my left. A T-shirt and a pair of trousers flapped on a clothesline out the back. The upper fields had been partitioned with thin white tape held by plastic stakes, so I figured someone was still living there. Three hundred metres further up on my right I came to a row of three flat, stone houses that sat low in the side of the hill, gazing down the valley. I knew from my map that this was Alpe Faller and these were the last houses before the Passo del Turlo. This was where Carl and his friends slept before crossing the pass.

The houses were open to the south with box-seat views down the Valsesia. Each of the houses had a small block of white quartz the size of a house brick standing on the apex of the roof ridge, a common feature of many of the mountain huts in the Valsesia. I was first told that these served as lightning conductors. I later learned a more compelling explanation: the blocks were placed on the roofs of country houses to ward off the *masche*. These evil beings are neither witches nor fairies but the spiteful spirits of women who, if displeased, have the power of ruination. If they want to, they can curdle the farmer's milk, render his cows dry or even cause them to abort their calves.

When the soldiers arrived at the Alpe Faller, they found the houses empty, the cattle having already been taken down in the valley to avoid the coming snow. Tired and cold, the soldiers forced their way into one of the huts. They were lucky to find cut wood, matches and a large copper pot. They decided to stay overnight and recover some strength before their last push to freedom. They had bags of rice and pasta that the good people of Riva Valdobbia had given them, which they decided to cook. The night was so cold that they over-stoked the fire and the chimney burst into flames. Fortunately, they were able to retrieve water from a nearby spring and dowse the fire before it spread. Peace restored, they settled down for a good night's sleep.

By the time I reached the Alpe Faller, the mist down in the valley had dispersed but the ridges high above me were still hidden under a heavy layer of clouds. The houses were just at the top of the tree line, around 2000 metres above sea level. As the path climbed on, the last larch trees and pastures gave way to barren slopes of rubble interspersed with tussocks of short coarse grass. The soil finished and the rocks began. The bare bones of the path were exposed. It rode over the top of the rubble on a solid foundation, the large, elongated stones fitting together like the pieces of a puzzle.

Although the route over the Passo del Turlo from Macugnaga to Alagna has been used for centuries, maybe more, the trail I walked was less than a hundred years old. Ever since Italy's unification in 1860, the new nation was preoccupied with securing its mountain passes against its northern neighbours. There was a perennial fear that the Austrians and Germans could violate Swiss neutrality and attack Italy through the valleys of the Valais and Engadine. This impulse was given fresh impetus in the 1920s when Mussolini came to power. The Passo del Turlo wasn't important enough to build a permanent fortification, but the Italian military wanted to be able to get mule-drawn cannons up here if required so the 4th Alpine Regiment was commissioned to build a transport road to the pass in the late 1920s.

Construction must have been brutal work. There was no shortage of raw materials on the spot. Granite blocks as large as small cars were strewn across the slopes. They were retrieved by hand, cut on site and dragged into position. The teams camped on the side of the mountain, only stopping work when the snow and conditions made it impossible to continue. It took six years to build the road up one side and down the other.

Neither the Austrians nor the Germans ever attacked Italy through Switzerland and the cannons were never needed. Ironically, the road served the Fascist regime's enemies best. It enabled the partisans to communicate with their leaders in Switzerland and to move combatants from one valley to another. It also allowed Jewish families and Allied prisoners of war to escape to safety.

After over seventy years of neglect, enduring snowstorms, landslides and avalanches, the *strada militare del Passo del Turlo* was still in pretty good condition, although, I imagined, not quite good enough for a mule-team dragging cannons to negotiate. In modern times the road has become a popular hiking route, part of the Tour de Monte Rosa, used by plenty of peaceful Austrians and Germans, uniting people rather than separating them.

By now the clouds had broken up and were lifting above the ridge. I could even see some blotches of blue behind the mist. After another forty minutes of climbing, I arrived at a small lake surrounded by deep snowdrifts. I dropped my pack and scrambled down to the closest one, keen to taste the August snow. It was icy and granular. I scratched it into a ball which I pressed to the back of my neck and then to my lips, sucking it until my lips started to tingle and go numb.

Above my head, a world of stone had opened up as the clouds receded, a sombre beauty that didn't inspire peace but rather strength and more than a little anxiety. Piles of broken rubble had accumulated at the bottom of the soaring cliffs. They seemed so precariously placed, interlocked like fiddle sticks, that if I displaced one, the whole mountain face would collapse and slide into the valley, taking me with it.

After passing the lake, the path steepened and climbed in tighter switchbacks, a ribbon of order across the chaos of the scree. It was my last push to the pass. By now I had been climbing for nearly three hours. I was exhausted. Staring at the trail, almost in a trance, I pushed my feet out one after the other with the uncertain steps of a toddler. As I had done before on the hike, I stopped every twenty metres or so, bent over and breathed deeply, my hands on my knees, my back bent, adjusting the straps of my backpack. Blue sky had broken through above the saddle I was climbing towards but I didn't seem to be getting any closer. I had to clamber over two sections where the retaining wall had collapsed and rocks had spilled over the road.

Finally, the road levelled slightly and cut back to the left and the top of the ridge was revealed. As I looked up, I noticed two curved horns moving against the blue sky. A large ibex, a cloven-hoofed mountain goat, regarded me from on high. A second, smaller one appeared beside it, the two of them surveying me, the curious guardians of that mineral world.

It was, of course, an omen. The ibex (capra ibex) is the symbol of the Alps, a mythological animal. They are only found above the tree line. They live in this stony world, eating grass and mosses where they can find them. The males can weigh over 100 kilos and have sweeping horns over a metre long, and yet they dance over the rocks like ballerinas and tippy-toe up the face of dams, looking for the salt that leeches out of the concrete.

It is very unlikely that Carl and his friends would have seen this wonderful sight. At the end of the war, Renzo Videsott, a ranger in the Valle d'Aosta and one of the saviours of the species, estimated that there were only 416 ibexes in the whole of the European Alps, and they were all located in the Cogne Valley, in the Valle d'Aosta, close to the French border.

Until the mid-nineteenth century, ibexes thrived throughout the Alps but with the introduction of modern weaponry, their numbers were decimated. The greatest hunter of all was Vittorio Emanuele II of Savoy, the future king of Italy, who slaughtered thousands of ibexes for trophies to adorn his palaces. The ibexes were also mercilessly hunted by the locals, who prized them for their meat, but also for their medicinal powers. The blood, for example, was believed to be a cure for conditions such as bronchitis and pleurisy as well as anaemia and blisters, not to mention the magical power of their horns.

In 1856, as numbers declined drastically, Vittorio Emanuele II declared a swathe of the Valle d'Aosta around Cogne as his own private hunting reserve and established a corps of gamekeepers to keep everyone else out. Only he was allowed to shoot there. He had seven hunting lodges built throughout the reserve, as well as over 300 kilometres of mule trails, wide enough to carry the sedan chair that transported him to and from the hunting grounds.

The king usually visited in the hot month of August. He hunted with a retinue of around 250 people that included porters and beaters, mostly locals. Once installed in his stone hide, the beaters would circle herds of ibex and drive them in towards the king, who blazed away. Behind him stood the *gran veneur* who would administer the *coup de grace* to the dying and wounded animals. Only mature males were killed, the females and young were left to grow and procreate. The king could kill several dozen in a single day's shooting. Sunday was the rest day. No killing. The parish priest came up from the valley to celebrate an open-air mass. The macabre decorations of the royal palace at Sarre,

Vittorio Emanuele's preferred residence in the mountains, 25 kilometres from Cogne, were created by the horns of over 3500 ibexes.

Despite these numbers, as the king was the only person who could hunt, the ibex population grew steadily. By 1919, the king's heirs had lost the taste for hunting, as well as the means to support such an indulgence, and they passed the reserve over to the Italian people. In 1922 the Parco Nazionale del Gran Paradiso was declared, the first national park in Italy. It held around 4000 ibexes, the only ones in the whole of the Alps. Their numbers plummeted again during World War II when the unguarded animals became easy prey for starving locals and German soldiers alike.

Post-war, action by committed volunteers like Renzo Videsott and various government entities ensured the survival of the species. So much so, that by the 1960s pairs of ibexes were introduced throughout the mountains of Italy and later into France, Switzerland and Austria. The ibex is no longer endangered. It is estimated that there are now over 47,000 roaming the high country of the Alps.

The ibexes on the Passo del Turlo stood calmly and looked down at me as if they didn't have a worry in the world, no hunters to be concerned about now. I waved them goodbye and pushed on up the path, keen to get to the pass.

The last stretch was the steepest, the edge of the trail plunging down on my left with vast views of the way I'd come. At the end of the climb, as the path curved right, I saw the opening of the pass, a cutting that connected the Valsesia with the Valle Quarazza. Three-and-a-half hours after leaving the Rifugio Pastore, I had arrived at the Passo del Turlo, 'the pass of the little door'.

On the left-hand side of the cutting was a worn marble plaque. On the top of the plaque was an imperial eagle perched on a globe that had the number 4 engraved in the middle. A nice bit of Fascist imagery to commemorate the work of the soldiers of the 4th Alpine Regiment. Beside the plaque, a deep niche had been cut into the stone. It was closed by a cast-iron grill with '1929' welded onto it. Locked behind the grill, in shadow, was a small statue of Mary draped in white: the Madonna della Neve, Our Lady of the Snow.

I was very pleased with myself for getting up here but, I'm sure, not as pleased as Carl and his mates must have been when they arrived at the pass seventy years earlier. Carl was a very religious man. He would have been comforted to see the Madonna protecting the pass but he would have been even more comforted by what he saw on the other side of the cutting: the long, uninhabited Quarazza Valley stretching away, far below. At the end of the valley, he would have seen the northern face of the Anzasca Valley. On the top of this wall, still hidden under cloud the day I was there, was the border to Switzerland.

I dropped my pack on the ground and slumped onto a stone bench under the niche. I had a long drink of water and pulled out my lunch pack. As I munched, I noticed a small tin box tucked inside the iron grill. I took out my pocketknife, opened the blade and slipped it through the grill, working the little box closer until I could reach it with my fingers and drag it under the bar. I popped it open. Inside was a water-stained exercise book and a pencil. I flipped through the pages. It was a log of people who had climbed to the pass. It wasn't great literature. It seemed that after the effort of getting up here, no one had the presence of mind to write anything profound. Most were satisfied to record the date, their names, their hometown and maybe a brief comment on the weather or the views. I was a bit more ambitious. While I chewed my panino, I tried to compose a fitting tribute to the generosity and courage of the people of these valleys, but the altitude defeated me too and I ended up simply writing the date, my name and country of origin and an exclamative comment about the views in Italian.

I had thought the worst of the day was behind me, but that wasn't so. I had covered 7 kilometres from the *rifugio* up to the pass. It was now midday, and I still had another 15 kilometres to go before getting to Macugnaga. There is something about the challenge and drama of climbing to the top that is intoxicating, but the descent is taken for granted, drudgery. Books are written about Hillary and Tenzing's ascent to the peak of Mount Everest, but no one is interested in the descent, which was probably more difficult. One conquers a mountain but never a valley. This is strange, because coming down can often be trickier than going up. When you climb, even walking up a path, you are leading with your eyes and hands, testing the surfaces before you place your feet. Gravity draws you into the slope. Going down is quite different. Your eyes are a long way from your boots, you can only guess at the surface underneath or the stability of the rock you are about to step on. On the way down, gravity pushes you out, away from the slope. You have to lean your torso back to counteract this, placing pressure on your knees. Your hands and arms are at best a counterbalance, flapping like wings as you slide downhill.

On the other side of the Passo del Turlo, the path swept around the side of a slope covered in a mass of large flat boulders and then curved out of sight to the left, seeming to fall off the edge of the cliff. Far below, the Valle Quarazza stretched north; a tiny aquamarine lake at the far end, Il Lago delle Fate, twinkled like a snake's eye.

I packed up my stuff and took the path, refreshed and keen to get to Macugnaga. The first section of the road was in excellent condition but once it started to drop, it quickly deteriorated, eroded by snow and neglect. Over the first rise, it worked its way down into the valley in a long series of tight zigzags. It took me over an hour to pick my way down the first 2 kilometres of the trail. The road finally levelled out. Washed away or buried, it became little more than a path, contouring around the right-hand side of the mountain. I turned and looked back at a vast colosseum of glacial debris. The 'pass of the little door' had disappeared behind an overhang. A waterfall, La Pissa, was crashing down the western side of the valley, and the peaks of Monte Rosa were still hidden under heavy clouds. I felt like an ant.

After another hour of now-easy walking, I came to a fork. I took the lower option that dropped down to the left and followed the twisting trail into dense scrub. The road here had long been deconstructed by the elements, turned into an obstacle course of ankle-cracking rocks. I concentrated on where I placed each foot but still managed to slip several times on the treacherous surface.

Finally, over two hours after leaving the pass, I came to the valley floor, greeted by half a dozen large cows grazing lazily on thick pasture beside the ruins of a stone hut. On the other side, the trail disappeared into thick pine forest and then wound along a stream. I thought I was on the home stretch but once again the trail deceived me. The gnarly limestone surface was solid but pitted and uneven. The pack swayed on my back as I placed one foot carefully in front of the other, indifferent to the pretty forest I was walking through. The sun had disappeared behind the ridge and long shadows slowly enveloped the valley. It was cooling down and I was sure I would never get to the end. I had seen the best. I was tired, fed up. It was now a monotonous grind, drudgery. All I wanted to do was get to the hotel, stop walking and have a cold beer.

After I had crossed several wooden bridges and walked past cascades and through woody glens, I came to a clearing, with several derelict buildings and a covered concrete pond the size of a large above-ground swimming pool, its sides stained by rust and leakage. A densely worded information panel nailed to a post in front of one of the buildings told me that I was in Crocette, *La Citta Morta,* the Dead City, which seemed a rather grand name for such a modest collection of buildings. I read on, glad for the break. Crocette had, in fact, been a mining settlement, people digging for the gold that was present in quartz veins high on the eastern slopes of the valley. There was archaeological evidence suggesting that the Celts and then the Romans had worked the deposits but it wasn't until 1892 that modern mining started. The gold was hard to get at, present in invisible flecks that had to be extracted through a complicated process of crushing and chemical treatment. The mining didn't get serious until 1936, when international boycotts against the Fascist government made it viable. Big investments were made. Electric cables were laid. Offices and accommodation were built, as were crushing and washing plants and chemical laboratories. Cable ways were connected to the mines that could bring down five tons of ore every hour but, even so, the venture was never sustainable. The mines were shut down in 1953. The company boarded up the buildings and walked away, a not uncommon practice in mining endeavours.

I walked across the path to the pool, a decaying cement structure 20 metres or so long, 10 metres wide and 2 metres high, covered with a heavy green tarpaulin. There was a clearer and more alarming sign nailed to the wall of the pool: *This area is heavily contaminated by toxic-noxious substances (in particular arsenic, mercury and cyanides which give the soils a blue colour) deriving from previous gold mining operations.*

Under this, in bold font, I was advised that, to protect my health, I should neither touch nor eat the earth in this area. It finished by stating that it was forbidden to take soil from the area; gather mushrooms, berries or other wild fruits; to camp or have picnics; graze cattle or cut hay.

Gold extraction is a dirty business involving very dangerous chemicals. Mercury is used to separate the gold from the pyrites, and potassium cyanide is then applied to purify the gold. On top of this toxic cocktail, arsenic occurs naturally in the pyrites. In the early 1980s, two cows grazing in this area were found dead – killed, as it turns out, by the poisons residual in the soil. The contaminated dirt was collected and enclosed in a reinforced concrete 'sarcophagus': the swimming pool I was standing in front of. Twenty years later, two horses died in the area, also killed by the lingering poisons. They were hastily buried, a cover-up, but it didn't take long for their decomposed carcasses to emerge from the soil. The shocked holidaymakers who found the remains reported it to the authorities. A scandal ensued. The mayor of Macugnaga sought to avoid bad publicity.

'Let's not exaggerate,' he said. 'This is something that has been going on for over a century. There is a drinking fountain near the sarcophagus and no one has ever reported any ill effects.' To appease public concern, a full investigation was initiated. Twelve years later, as I stood before the decaying pool, the results of the report were still pending.

There are some, more pleasing, stories about the mines, however. The legend goes that there are gnomes, *gut viarghini* in the local dialect, who live nearby and work the mines at night. They give the gold they find to the fairies who live on the shores of the lake at the end of the valley. In exchange for the gold, the gnomes receive blueberry jam, of which they are particularly fond. The fairies use the gold to embroider their clothes and to make the magic dust that enables them to fly. As they flap their wings, some of the dust falls off, floating on the surface of the lake, causing the water to sparkle in the sun. I hoped that the authorities had advised the gnomes of the dangers inherent in these practices.

The best thing to come out of Crocette was the unsealed road that the mining company had put through the forest to connect the mines with the village at the end of the valley. It was a great relief to finally be able to relax, to look at the forest around me rather than the uneven rocks I had been walking on for the last three hours. I realised that I was getting close to the end when a jogger and a couple wearing sneakers passed me by.

When the road left the forest, I took a path that went up to the right and followed it along a grassy embankment above the stream. I stopped and turned to look again to where I had come from. The head of the valley, 6 kilometres south, was closed by a black wall, streaked with patches of snow. Torn grey clouds sat on the ridge obscuring the flank of Monte Rosa on the right but I imagined I could just make out the Passo del Turlo high on the left.

I shortly hit civilisation, arriving at a small restaurant that thankfully was open. On the other side of the path, perched on a levy, was a row of umbrellas, sunchairs and tables overlooking Il Lago delle Fate, the Lake of the Fairies.

It would have been a very different scene when Carl and his friends arrived on the evening of 2 October 1943. There would have been no lake back then. The lake had been built by a private company to generate hydroelectricity in 1952, the year before the gold mines closed. The stream would have run, uninterrupted, all the way down to meet the Anza River. There would have been no restaurant and certainly no sunchairs and umbrellas. Instead, the men would have been walking into the small hamlet of Quarazza. The hamlet was submerged in 1952 when the lake was formed. The only remnant to survive was a chapel, the village church that had been deconstructed and rebuilt on higher ground, up around the corner from the restaurant.

A pre-war sepia photo of Quarazza shows a dozen simple Walser houses scattered up the slope. In the 1940s, four families lived in Quarazza. They were farmers and cowherds. Some of them also worked in the gold mines above Crocette. For generations, members of the families who lived in Quarazza supplemented their meagre incomes by moonlighting as *contrabbandieri*, smugglers, who carried goods back and forth over the nearby Swiss border.

The earliest document that mentions smuggling in these parts dates from the early 1600s. The smugglers were known as *spalloni* (big shoulders) because of the large packs they carried on their backs, which held up to 40 kilos of goods. They took rice, wine and other foodstuffs into Switzerland and brought back tax-free medicines, coffee, salt and, especially, cigarettes, delivering them to agents who waited on either side of the border. Both men and women were involved. It was poorly paid and dangerous work, but they were desperate times. The borders were patrolled by armed guards so the *spalloni* had to stay off the established trails: the more dangerous the path, the less likely they were to be caught. They climbed high into the mountains with poor equipment (a pair of farm boots and a long staff), heavy loads tied to their backs with rope. They usually travelled at night without lights, in any weather conditions. Each 'run' took around twenty hours. Some people did it two or three times a week. Accidents were common. In February 1933, eight *spalloni* from the nearby village of Crodo lost their lives in an avalanche. Their bodies weren't recovered until the following spring thaw.

Smuggling in these border areas had died out by the 1970s when the towns began to experience the benefits of Italy's post-war 'economic miracle' but I was told that most of the businesses in Macugnaga, and similar border towns, had been established on money earned by smuggling.

Once a source of embarrassment and shame, in a generation smuggling had become a source of pride, evidence of the ingenuity and resilience of these mountain communities. Macugnaga now has a small museum celebrating the subject and they enjoy telling 'shaggy dog' stories about the 'cat and mouse' games that went on between the *contrabbandieri* and the customs officer.

After 8 September 1943, when Italy switched sides, the *contrabbandieri* turned into *passatori*, or guides, the smugglers now using their knowledge and skills to help the Jewish families and Allied POWs who came down the valleys to escape to safety on the other side of the border. Sometimes they asked for money or goods but often they did it for free, out of the goodness of their hearts. One of the centres was in Quarazza.

Elated at having reached the Passo del Turlo, Carl and his friends dropped down into the Quarazza Valley, following the same trail I had, no doubt avoiding the mines at Crocette, which would still have been operating at the time. In the woods just outside Quarazza, near where the restaurant now stood, they approached the first houses of the hamlet where they were met by a teenage boy who offered to guide them over the mountains into Switzerland in exchange for their watches and greatcoats. It was a good deal. Carl believed that this boy was their saviour. He must have been a very brave, or a very desperate, young man. He told the group that his brother had been shot by a German patrol shortly before this while guiding another group of POWs over the passes. The boy accompanied them into the hamlet and took them to a barn, where they were given a feed of boiled potatoes and told to rest up.

In 2013, Angelo Iachinni, a former resident of Quarazza, was interviewed by Turin's *La Stampa* newspaper about this lost village. When he was growing up in the 1930s, Angelo said, Quarazza was an oasis of total peace, but everything changed on 8 September 1943 with the daily arrival of people headed for Switzerland. Angelo became a *passatore*. There were people of all ages and types coming through: Jews, Allied POWs and the politically persecuted. During the day they were hidden in the barns, but in the evening a great animation began for the departure, favoured by the falling of night. He remembered them all well. Angelo said that he lived with his family in the house closest to the mountain, which would have been the first house the POWs encountered when they arrived in the hamlet. Angelo was born in 1927 and would have been sixteen in 1943. He was working in the nearby gold mines when the Germans occupied the valley. Was he the guide who led Carl and his friends to safety? Very possibly but, unfortunately, I didn't get a chance to ask him. Angelo died in November 2016, aged eighty-nine.

I was very tempted to have a beer at the little restaurant and sit in a sunchair to admire the view over the lake but I knew that would have been a mistake. As close as I was to the end of my hike, I still had the best part of an hour of walking ahead of me. Instead, I lined up at the little service window and ordered a gelato, a single scoop of lemon sorbet, and kept going along the unsealed road, out of the Quarazza Valley. Despite the weight of my backpack, my stiff calf muscles and my now aching feet, I felt happy, relieved at being close to the end.

At the top of a rise, I passed the small chapel that had been saved from flooding and then picked up a road that curved down to the left and entered the Valle Anzasca, a long valley that ran from the town of Piedimulera in the east, near Lake Maggiore, to the foot of Monte Rosa in the west. I passed through dappled forest, birch trees climbing up the hill on the left, their outstretched limbs casting dancing shadows over the smooth gravel road and larch pines on my right that ran down to the Anza River. Beyond the river was a high rock wall, the north side of the valley, at the top of which ran the Swiss border. As I walked, I caught glimpses of clusters of Walser houses sitting on bulges above the riverbanks.

Macugnaga, the town I was heading for, doesn't actually exist. It is a bureaucratic construct, a name covering five villages that stretch along the Anza River at the base of the mountain. In ascending order up the valley from east to west, they are Motta, Borca, Staffa, Precetto and Dorf. Dorf is the oldest, the first settlements that the Walsers made after they had crossed the Monte Moro Pass in the thirteenth century. It was from here that they pushed south, crossing over the Passo del Turlo to Alagna and then into the Valsesia. Titsch, their dialect, is still commonly spoken today in Macugnaga, particularly amongst the older people.

After thirty minutes, I came down to the banks of the Anza River, where the valley widened, opening up to the small flood plain where the villages of Staffa and Precetto had grown. The bridge I had planned to cross, a short cut into town, had been taken out by floods the previous spring so I had to walk further uphill, continuing through the forest for another kilometre until I came to a smaller footbridge that had survived the floods. I crossed the river and walked past vegetable allotments, down into the old town, the snow-scattered peak of Monte Moro rising behind me.

I took La Ripa Vecchia, a small lane, past timber houses to the main road and then arrived at my destination, the Hotel Zumstein, named after the fourth-highest peak on Monte Rosa, a modern four-storey hotel built in generic Walser style, timber veneer and geranium-filled flowerboxes.

I fell in love with the hotel as soon as I stepped through the entrance. A large wooden gnome seated on a red toadstool stood guard at the door. The interior décor was full 1960s. The hotel was empty and exuded an atmosphere of calm, a feeling of relief at having arrived at the end of another summer season. There was a bar on my right. Beyond this was an elegant cocktail lounge, closed for the interregnum. To the left of the entrance was the reception.

An elderly lady, barely tall enough to see over the desk, smiled at me as I walked in. 'Signor Tancred,' she stated rather than asked.

I handed her my passport, which she thumbed through thoughtfully and then placed in a pigeonhole. She took down an old-fashioned bit key, which swung at the end of a large chunk of wood, and slid it across to my outstretched hand. My room was on the second floor; a double bed, nice and long. I thanked her and asked her politely if I could possibly have a glass of beer. Of course, she declared, and rang a buzzer under the counter.

After a minute, an elderly gentleman pulling on a jacket came shuffling up the hall. He smiled amiably and invited me to follow him into the bar. He squeezed himself behind the counter and fished around underneath until he found a longneck of Menabrea. He knocked the top off and slowly half-filled a glass stein, creating a nice frothy head. He passed both to me. 'You'll need that, I'm sure,' he said.

I sat over in one of the cubicles and took a long, hard pull at the beer.

'*Salut!*' he added with another smile as he watched me drain the glass and fall back into the embrace of the thickly padded seat.

His wife, Signora Sandra, tottered over and sat on a stool by the bar and we chatted about the walk I had just done. I retold the tale of Carl and his friends. Unlike most of the people I had spoken with along the way, they were very familiar with the story.

'We both grew up during the war,' Sandra said. 'We were

only small children, but we have strong memories of those times. We knew all about the *passatori* and their adventures getting the refugees to safety over the mountain. They were all around us. The border guards and the smugglers were neighbours. It was a game of chess. In the evenings they would sit down and have drinks together but no one would say anything. They never talked about their work.'

Signora Sandra told me that apart from the border patrols, the German occupation had not been heavy-handed. 'They were quite polite,' she said, 'and went about their business without causing too much trouble.'

Like the people in the Valle Vogna, I suspected that this coexistence had something to do with their shared traditions and their shared languages. I'm guessing the Germans considered the people of the valley part of the Pan German diaspora and went easy on them.

I thanked them for their company and then climbed the stairs up to my second-floor room where I found my suitcase lying on a rack in the corner, bursting with clean clothes. For a reasonable sum, I had organised a driver to bring the bag around from Biella. It had been money well spent.

I sat on the edge of the large bed and unlaced my boots. I placed the malodorous footwear, boots and socks at the far end of my balcony and quickly closed the door behind me. I stripped off and took a long hot shower. Dried off, I wrapped myself in a full-length, fluffy white bathrobe and flopped onto the soft bed. I lay there, head propped on thick feather pillows and looked out the window, wallowing in the luxury.

The *signora* had recommended dinner at the Taverna del Rosa and had rung ahead to book a table for me. It was a short walk up the hill, she told me. To get there, I followed her suggestion and took a short cut across a vacant lot and then walked up the hill past more wooden houses. The trattoria was a free-standing stone building with its back to the Monte Moro pass. It had Pompeii red window shutters and a wide stone patio lined with rows of flowerboxes filled with gay geraniums. The trattoria was opposite the funicular that went up to the Monte Moro Pass, the Swiss border and the end of my hike.

Following the *signora*'s other recommendation, before having my dinner, I carried on up the road past the trattoria to Dorf, the smallest, highest and oldest village of Macugnaga, a handful of timber houses and barns gathered around the Chiesa Vecchia, the Old Church. Dorf stands at the head of the Valle Anzasca, completely enclosed by mountains, glaciers stretching down towards it on two sides. It was here that the stone path down from Monte Moro finished. It was here that the first Walser arrived, founding their first settlement south of the Valais, and it was from here that I planned to start my climb up to the pass the following morning.

The Chiesa Vecchia is a small, simple church with white-washed walls and a tall stone belltower. The first record of the church is in a document dated from 1317. It was rebuilt in the early 1500s and the belltower was added later in the same century. One hundred years further on, as the settlement grew, the Chiesa Vecchia was superseded by a new, bigger parish church down at Staffa, but its importance still remains.

Inside the church is a statue of the Madonna of the Glaciers. Every July, she is carried in procession through the streets of Macugnaga to ensure that the town is protected from the caprices of the mountain for another year, a hangover from the Middle Ages when the advancing glacier was a real threat.

Behind the church, enclosed by a low stone wall, are rows of carefully tended graves, a number of them with freshly cut flowers. This graveyard is known as the 'mountaineers' cemetery'. It is the final resting place of many of the town's heroes. The greatest of these is Ferdinand Imseng, who led the first ascent of the east face of Monte Rosa in 1872.

Ferdinand was born in Saasfee on the Swiss side of Monte Moro but he was raised in Macugnaga. As a young man he worked in the gold mines where he met three English tourists, William Martin Pendlebury, his brother Richard and a friend. It was the heroic age of Alpine mountaineering and the three Englishmen were planning to conquer a mountain and were looking for a local guide to help them. They convinced young Ferdinand to take them up Monte Rosa. They took on the east side, the most daunting face of the mountain. Their success launched Macugnaga as a mountaineering destination. In 1881, an avalanche killed Ferdinand and two companions. Their remains have never been found, probably obliterated by the torrent of ice and rocks. He is remembered by a brief epithet on a raw block of granite in the cemetery: *Bonne guide, honnète homme* (Good guide, honest man).

In front of the church, also surrounded by a low stone wall, is a large linden tree (Tilia platyphyllos), a deciduous native, whose abundant heart-shaped leaves were just starting to turn. It is a large tree, 18 metres high with a girth of nearly 8 metres, and it is the symbol of the community of Macugnaga. According to legend, this linden tree was planted in the second half of the thirteenth century by a young woman who was part of the first founding Walser settlers. She had carried the tiny seedling, barely a span high, as a *trait-d'union*, a hyphen, a connection between the new settlement and their Valaisan homeland to the north. Community meetings, annual fairs, weddings and judicial hearings were held under the tree's branches until recently. The legend goes that *gut viarghini*, the same little gnomes who worked the gold mines in the Valle Quarazza, lived in the branches of this tree, dispensing wise counsel to the magistrates of Macugnaga. One day they were teased by some nasty children because of their misshapen feet, at which they took great offence. They disappeared in a huff, taking their good counsel with them, and have never been seen since.

It was dark by the time I headed back down Via Chiesa Vecchia to the Taverna del Rosa. I walked into a dark and crowded bar. A tall woman with a rich, deep voice greeted me and led me through to the cosy dining room, its timber-lined walls illuminated by sconces and decorated with copper kitchenware. A small fire was burning in the corner. The lady seated me at a table covered with heavy linen. She removed the other settings, placed a large menu in front of me and asked me what I would like to drink. I ordered still water and a carafe of local red prunent, a variation of the Nebbiolo grape. I ordered as Signora Sandra had instructed: *focaccia al lardo, fondue chinoise* and a large serve of fried potato chips. I had no idea what to expect. It didn't sound all that healthy so I offset it with a green salad. My host was very pleased with the order and asked me to send her regards to the *signora*.

The focaccia arrived first, my antipasto. It was a large crunchy white pizza covered in strips of lard, not the boiled down 'dripping' my father ate in the Great Depression, but thin slivers of the fatty cut of a leg of prosciutto, heavily salted and impregnated with wild herbs.

I only sent back a couple of wedges, with my apologies to the chef. 'Saving space for the rest of the meal,' I explained to the waitress.

I sat back and pretended to read my book, happy to eavesdrop on the conversations around me. My host arrived with another waitress and began to prepare my table. First, she set a round ceramic plate with six compartments in front of me, on which she placed a long thin fork with a wooden handle. Next came a tray with half a dozen dipping sauces. This was followed by another large plate, covered in paper-thin slices of bright red beef. As the other diners looked on, the lady cleared the middle of the table while her colleague carried out the last piece of equipment, a large steel pot of simmering broth, an oil flame flickering in a small burner underneath it. My heart sank. Not what I had been hoping for, but I smiled politely and feigned enthusiasm.

Without asking, she picked up a couple of the sauces, spooned dollops into each of the compartments of my plate and then snagged a slice of beef, furling it around the fork and dipped it into the broth.

'It should be ready in a minute or two,' she explained.

'And when it is, you put it into the sauces. *Et voilà!* She smiled proudly, adjusted the flame and stood back.

Just as I was about to take the beef out, the swinging door to the kitchen slapped open and a burly man came out holding a large plate of deep fried, hand-cut potato chips.

'I grew these potatoes myself,' he told me as he placed them in front of me.

I slid the curled beef onto the plate, cut it in half and dipped one half into a mayonnaise-based sauce. It was delicious. Tender, melt in your mouth, the tang of the spicy broth enveloped by the buttery sauces. The potatoes were excellent as well. I topped up my glass and settled in, savouring each mouthful and feeling a deep sense of satisfaction. There was still tomorrow's climb, but I was close to the end, mission almost accomplished.

It was a memorable meal. The only dud note was the green salad, which was taken away untouched. By this point in the hike, I felt a meal wouldn't be complete without a bowl of *bunet*, so I ordered a large serving, once again with my host's full approval.

Restored, I wandered back down the unlit lane to my hotel and let myself in through a side door. I reached over the reception counter to retrieve my room key. An old paperback had been slipped into the pigeonhole beside the key. There was a yellow post-it note stuck to the cover: 'Tancred. I thought you might be interested in this. Sandra.'

I flipped the book over. Written in bold red capitals at the top of the white front cover was the author's name, Elsa Oliva, and then under this, also in red capitals, the title of the book: *Ragazza Partigiana* (The Girl Partisan). Below the title was a black-and-white photo of a group of twenty-somethings, gathered in the snow. They all seemed to be laughing. Eight men and three women. Seated in the middle of the group sat a pretty young woman wearing a peaked Lenin cap and a radiant smile – the author, Elsa Oliva. It could have been *gita fuori porta*, a weekend away, except that Elsa and the woman sitting beside her were both carrying submachine guns.

The cover was stained with time and use. I opened to the front page and saw that it was published in Novara in 1969. I then turned to the blurb on the back cover. The book, it told me, was about the adventurous life of Elsa Oliva, who was born in 1921. She was a painter and committed anti-Fascist, who joined the partisan resistance first in the Beltrami Alpine Brigade and then in the Franco Abrami Brigade. She was intrepid and courageous, and she wanted to be an armed and active frontline combatant, not just a supporter. Her story is one of the few stories of women involved in the resistance that is still remembered today. This is a sad fact.

Women were a fundamental element in the resistance against the Nazi–Fascist regime. Women found and delivered the food, medical supplies and other resources that sustained the partisans in the mountains. Women organised anti-Fascist propaganda, raised funds and gave assistance to political prisoners. Their most famous role, however, was as *staffette*, messengers who ran the despatches that maintained communication between the different partisan groups and between their supporters and families.

The job of a *staffetta* was basically to be invisible, to pass by unobserved, and as a result this role often fell to young women, girls aged between sixteen and eighteen, who attracted less suspicion and usually avoided checks and patrols. Apart from transporting messages, food, medicines and weapons, the *staffette* often worked as scouts, monitoring and reporting on enemy movements. When a partisan unit arrived near a town, it was the *staffetta* who first entered the town to make sure there were no enemies and to give the partisans the OK to continue their advance. It was, of course, extremely dangerous work. The *staffette* were not armed and, if captured, they were often subjected to appalling torture and execution.

Many women became active combatants as well, some ending up as leaders of partisan units. Nineteen women were awarded the Medaglia d'Oro, Italy's highest award for bravery. According to one estimate, up to 35,000 women fought on the front line. Elsa Oliva was one of them.

I crept up the stairs of the darkened hotel to my room. It was still early. I sat on my bed and unfolded the next day's map. The climb up to the Monte Moro Pass from Macugnaga was as steep and as high, 1500 metres, as the climb I did up to Rifugio Rivetti, and I remembered how that had ended.

There were two trails leading to the pass, one that started at the Chiesa Vecchia and one that started back down the river. They joined about halfway up the mountain. There was also the cable-car, so I had three options. As I had peeled off my boots on my arrival at the hotel, I had been very tempted by the cable-car but, after the long hot shower and a second beer down at the bar, I had decided that I had to finish the job properly. Besides, I was fitter than when I had started and, best of all, I could leave my 12-kilo backpack in the hotel and hike with just a daypack.

The most obvious way up to the Monte Moro Pass was the historic path that started at the Chiesa Vecchia. It had been the main thoroughfare to and from Switzerland for centuries. The alternative route was a mule trail taking farmers up to the small patches of high pasture in the summer. This trail wound up through forest to Alpe Meccia and then on to Alpe Sonobierg before coming out above the tree line, halfway up the mountain. It then cut across the bare slopes to join the historic path for the final push up to the pass. I was confident this smaller trail would have been the trail that Carl and his friends had taken. Firstly, it was less visible, hidden in the forest for more than half the way. Secondly, it would have been less trafficked. Thirdly, it started further down the river, which meant that it avoided the centre of town, and it was closer to Quarazza, from where they set out.

I put the maps away, tucked myself into my very comfortable bed, switched on the light on the bedside table, and started reading about the *ragazza partigiana*.

It was simply written, the language essential and immediate. The book was full of stories of derring-do. Elsa writes about the great courage and endurance of her companions and the love and endless respect she had for them and the people who took enormous risks to support the partisans. It burns with contempt for the Fascists and their Nazi allies.

Elsa Oliva was born into an anti-Fascist family in Piedimulera at the beginning of the Valle Anzasca on 11 April 1921. She was the third of seven brothers and sisters. In 1930, when she was nine years old, her father lost his job because he refused to sign up to the local Fascist party, and Elsa was forced to abandon school to go to work as a servant in a wealthy family. She was a restless, rebellious child. Dissatisfied with this life, when she was fourteen she ran away with her fifteen-year-old brother Renato and started life in the Valsesia. They supported themselves by painting and selling landscapes and portraits of people in the street.

They eventually returned to their home in Domodossola. Following her father's influence, Elsa became a committed, and active, anti-Fascist.

In 1942, Elsa was arrested and sent into exile in Ortisei, a small town in the Dolomite mountains close to the Austrian border, where she worked in a wood-painting workshop. She moved to Bolzano, where she worked at the municipal registry office until 8 September 1943, when she became an active part of the resistance. She defended the barracks from an attack by the occupying Germans, helping to organise the escape of the Italian soldiers who were interned inside, providing them with false documents, and then destroying the registry archive so as not to leave traces of her actions.

Elsa continued her anti-Fascist activities. One night, in the streets of Bolzano, she shot and killed a German officer who was molesting her, but managed to escape unseen. She was eventually arrested in November. She was interrogated and accused of being a 'rebel', a term she embraced.

Elsa managed to escape from the train that was transporting her north to Innsbruck to be tried. She found her way back to Domodossola, the city near her hometown of Piedimulera, where her parents had moved.

Hunted by the SS, in May 1944 Elsa joined the partisans of the second brigade of the Beltrami Division, first as a nurse and then, later, becoming a front-line fighter, taking the *nom de guerre* Elsinki, Helsinki in English. She was twenty-three.

In October, she left the Beltrami Division and joined another brother, Aldo, in a different division, the Banda Liberta. Eight months later, Aldo, the 'original rebel' as Elsa described him, was shot by the Fascists in Carcegna, a small town on Lake Maggiore, betrayed for a bounty by a companion.

On 8 December, Elsa was captured and taken to Omegna. Certain to be shot, she simulated suicide, ingesting a large dose of sleeping pills that had been smuggled into her room. The Fascists couldn't execute a sick person so she was taken to a hospital to recover for her execution. After a stomach pump, and with the help of a doctor, Giuseppe Annichini, and a nun, Sister Augusta, Elsa managed to escape. Back in action, she changed groups again, joining the Franco Abrami Brigade, which was based on Mount Mottarone, overlooking Lago Maggiore. Elsa became the commander of one of the units, which took on her *nom de guerre* and was known as the Volante Elsinki, the Helsinki Flying Squad. Mottarone became the scene of particularly bitter fighting in November 1944 when 8000 Nazi–Fascist soldiers pushed into the mountain, determined to destroy the partisan forces. After the liberation, Elsa received the rank of lieutenant.

At the end of *Ragazza Partigiana*, on 25 April 1945, the day before she 'descends to the plains' to join Cino Moscatelli's forces as they march triumphant into Milan, twenty-five-year-old Elsa reflected on her future and was almost nostalgic for the fighting life she was leaving behind.

Before marching to Milan, she visited a small cemetery to say goodbye to her brother and some companions who were buried there. She sat on the edge of her brother's grave and thought for a long time about what would become of her in the future. She felt at peace up there and was reluctant to leave. Almost with trepidation, she walked down the rocky dirt road, out of the mountains and down towards the plains. She was in no hurry to get there. The next day, she would be walking on the road to victory, the same road that her brother Aldo had dreamed of walking.

Elsa remained active politically until the 1970s, including a spell as a Communist Party representative on the Domodossola municipal council. Disillusioned with this experience, she broke away from the party shortly after completing her first term and withdrew from politics. She died in Domodossola on 11 April 1994.

Elsa Oliva was a hero. She was the archetypal partisan: young, courageous and decisive. It was because of the likes of her that Italy emerged from the humiliation of twenty years of Fascist rule and the ruins of World War II and recreated itself as a modern democratic republic.

Above: Monte Rosa from the Passo di Monte Moro.

Below: Monte Rosa from the Valle Anzasca.

CHAPTER 8

Macugnaga to Passo di Monte Moro
7 kilometres, 1500-metre ascent, 5 hours

I had an early breakfast, avoiding the hawk eyes of the rather unpleasant waitress as I stuffed the usual provisions into my daypack: two panini with cheese and ham plus two pieces of fruit. I left the hotel and headed down the hill towards the main square.

Carl and his mates had a much earlier start than me. They were woken up at 2 o'clock in the morning of 3 October 1943 when the youth came to collect them. It was an early winter, and the weather would have been bitterly cold. The boy brought them some acorn coffee that had been laced with *génépi*, a fiery liquid made from wormwood. In single file and in complete silence, the men left the hamlet and followed the boy along a narrow path through a pine forest towards Macugnaga, the Anzasca River roaring in the darkness below them. The boy signalled them to stay still and disappeared down the path. He returned ten minutes later, breathing heavily and smiling. Through a mash of Italian and English, he was able to tell them that for some reason, providence perhaps, the guards had been taken off the bridge and they could now cross it, avoiding having to wade through the freezing and treacherous waters of the river.

I had decided to do the walk as closely as possible to the way Carl and his friends had done it, and so, after leaving the hotel, I headed downhill, crossed the main square and walked down to the bridge where I picked up the trail. I followed it back uphill as it wrapped around some boarded-up Walser houses. Just before the square, I took a short cut up to the main road. On the other side, the path dived in behind more houses, eventually coming out at a large street lined with handsome holiday homes surrounded by manicured gardens, Via delle Ville. These were obviously new developments that would not have existed seventy years ago. It probably would have been fenced pastures back then.

To the left of a pair of imposing granite pillars, a small yellow sign pointed to a narrow grassy trail that climbed uphill into woodland, the beginning of my ascent to the Passo di Monte Moro, the soldiers' climb to freedom. It was a long, steady haul up a small trail, a narrow line of flagstones weaving through larch pines. The forest was scattered with lichen-stained granite boulders embedded in a floor of thick moss and pine needles.

This was the last and the longest climb of Carl's odyssey, over 1500 metres straight up to the pass. The men were shattered and struggled to make their way along the slippery path, clinging to the pine trees to pull themselves up as they went. They stopped regularly to catch their breath. The boy was nimble and only Carl was able to keep up with him. The two of them would pause regularly to allow the others to catch up with them, but as soon as they did, Carl and the boy set off again. Time was critical. They had to get as far up the mountain as possible before the sun rose and the guards down in the valley would begin scanning the mountains and the passes for escapees.

After an hour of steady climbing, there was a break in the trees and I came to a clearing with the ruins of two stone houses, Alpe Meccia. High above me I could see the pass, with the grey stone pyramid of Monte Moro rising above this on the left. There was still a long way to go.

Staffa was visible far below, a toy town silently going about its morning business. Across the river, the pointed black mass of Pizzo Bianco rose above the town. Monte Rosa peered over its shoulder, completely covered in thick snow.

There was a simple marble plaque attached to a boulder below one of the houses. It commemorated the Martyrs of Meccia. On 22 October 1944, a year after Carl and his friends had passed through, a group of young partisans were killed here. Under the plaque, there was a list of the names and ages of the victims, eight men and two women, all in their early to mid-twenties. Early on that October morning, as dawn broke, a local man, a traitor, had led Nazi troops silently up the same path that I had just climbed. The troops had surrounded the two huts and started firing without warning, giving the partisans no chance to surrender. One of the women killed was pregnant. Only two partisans escaped, managing to burst out of the door and roll down a nearby gully in the confusion.

I carried on to Alpe Sonobierg, passing another memorial to the Martyrs of Meccia. It was a wooden panel nailed to a pine tree up above the path. The handwritten dedication read: *To all the partisans who died for a future of peace hope and dignity 22.10.1944.* Below this was a declaration by Don Sisto Bighiani: *On your knees to pray, on your feet to fight.*

Don Sisto Bighiani was not your usual priest. He was born in 1920 into a Walser family in Ornovasso, south of Domodossola. Even while he was studying in the seminary in Novara to become a priest, Don Sisto was collaborating with the local partisans, many of whom were his friends and contemporaries. This included smuggling weapons and ammunition with the help of the boys from the oratory and Caritas. On 28 May 1944, Don Sisto was celebrating his ordination as a priest in his uncle Carlo's tavern when there was pounding at the door. It was a raid by the Fascist military in search of the new priest. The taverna was trashed and two people killed but Don Sisto managed to escape. He took to the mountains above his town where he joined the Patrioti d'Italia Brigade, a predominantly Catholic group.

In July, for reasons not clear, he left this group and joined the Communist-led Garibaldi Brigade in the neighbouring Valsesia (Sesia Valley), which was under the command of Cino Moscatelli – the Communist Party a very unusual choice for a priest as the communists were avowed atheists and anti-clerics. Don Sisto earned the respect of Moscatelli and was eventually appointed political commissar of the brigade. The political commissar was a role that was invented by the Bolsheviks in 1918. Its function was as a supervisory officer responsible for the political education and organisation of the unit to which they were assigned, with the intention of ensuring political control of the military. Don Sisto had the distinction of being the only minister of God in Italy to occupy such a position.

After the war, when asked about this strange conjunction, Don Sisto said there was no conflict in the roles: just as a priest forms the souls and guides the development of his flock, so the commissar educates and guides the fighters, explaining the reasons they are resisting Fascism and helping them along the path to democracy. Don Sisto was at the head of the column of partisans from the Valsesia, led by Cino Moscatelli, who victoriously entered Milan on 26 April 1945. The resistance leadership's respect for Don Sisto was such that he was invited to address the crowds in Milan's Piazza Duomo.

A complicated figure for the church hierarchy, after the war had finished, Don Sisto was made parish priest of the tiny, isolated village of Macugnaga. He rode his bicycle there from Ornovasso and spent the rest of his short life dedicated to the community of this small town. He died in a car crash in 1979, aged fifty-nine.

An hour after leaving the Alpe Meccia, the path emerged from the forest and met the main trail leading up to the Passo di Monte Moro. Somewhere at this point, Carl and his friends parted ways with the boy. Their young guide hung back in the forest and refused to go any further. He was worried that the Germans down in the valley would be able to spot him with their field glasses and would pick him up when he returned to his village. The boy pointed up to the beautiful mountains that rose above them and said, 'There is Switzerland.' The men gave the boy their watches and greatcoats, as agreed, and then started their final climb. After nearly three years in hell, they were two hours from freedom.

The larch pines gave way to low scrub, prickly green juniper bushes and low tussocks of Alpine sedge. The main route zigzagged steeply up towards the pass. I set off as well, following not only in the steps the Walser settlers had trodden 800 years ago but also treading on the same stones that Carl and his mates had traversed seventy years earlier.

After another half an hour, I stopped to catch my breath and look at the spectacle around me. The blue morning sky was disappearing as clouds closed in, catching on the ragged crests. Drifts of snow lay in gullies above me, a reminder that winter never leaves these mountains.

Carl also admired the 'beautiful' sight, but he didn't dwell. There was still some serious climbing to go before they would be safe.

I had been going well to this point, excited by the final climb, pleased not to be carrying my backpack. However, once on the main trail, the pain had returned; a week of hiking had taken its toll. My legs were heavy, my steps slow. The closer I got to the peak, the steeper the path seemed to become. Near the top, the path entered a world of shattered stone. Over the ages, snow and ice seemed to have crushed the ridge, dragging the broken stratum of granite down the slope, dumping it in a chaotic mess. The path wound through this rubble. I squeezed through a narrow defile created by two leaning erratics and realised I was finally at the top.

On the other side of the erratics, the path had levelled out. A small cable-car suspended on a very thin wire scooted overhead. I came to a post with two large yellow signs. One pointed to the left, directing me to the cable-car station and the *rifugio*. I followed the second one and kept going straight ahead until I came to a small lake. Beyond it was a large, flat slab of sloping granite. Crude wooden stairs with a looping chain handrail led up the side of the slab. At the top was a distant golden statue of the Madonna delle Nevi, Our Lady of the Snows. She stood splendidly on a granite plinth surrounded by snow, 2950 metres above sea level. She marked the Italian–Swiss border: the end of my hike.

It would have been a very different scene for Carl and his friends. For a start, the Madonna would not have been there. She was installed in August 1966, funded by the local funicular company hoping that her dazzling form would draw tourists to the pass. The *rifugio*, cable station and scrappy pylons wouldn't have been there either, just the rubble.

I was very tired. It had been the longest and steepest climb of the entire hike. I kicked the toes of my boots into the snow, took hold of the chain and pulled myself up the wooden stairs. My right calf ached, my feet throbbed, I had to stop at every second step to recapture the air that the altitude had stolen from me and I was starting to get a headache, but, despite all this, I was very happy. I had made it.

At the top, I flopped with my back against the base of the Madonna and looked around. To my left, on the other side of the valley, was the sawtooth ridge that separated Valsesia from the Valle Anzasca. I was sure I could make out the Passo del Turlo and below this the folds of the Valle Quarazza. In front of me, the bulging black mass of the Pizzo Bianco, Macugnaga invisible at its feet. Looming over all of this was the east face of Monte Rosa, with Punta Gnifetti on the left of the massif and Punta Nordend on the right, the two peaks sweeping up like the horns of the devil.

At the base of the mountain, a great river of dirty grey ice, the Monte Rosa glacier, curved around under the Pizzo Bianco, split in two by the Crestone Marinelli, each flow tapering to a point like the forked tongue of a snake, pointing down the valley towards Macugnaga. It was a magnificent view that Carl and his friends would have at last been able to appreciate. It was also their last glimpse of Italy. They were almost untouchable.

꧁ ꧂

I unclipped my photo of Uncle John from my daypack and planted it in the snow. I sat back and imagined him clambering up to the ridge where I was sitting. He, too, is tired, exhausted, but exhilarated by the freedom that is so close he can almost touch it. No chains and stairs for him, no Madonna, just the big, bare granite boulders, patched with snow, that he has to negotiate. He gets to the top, reaches down a hand to his mate. They stand on the ridge and look down into the deep, bare Saastal, the Saas Valley, Switzerland. Free at last! He flops down and sits on a rock, panting heavily. He and his mates shake hands and slap each other on the back.

'We fucking made it!' he shouts, as much to himself as to them.

But he's not quite ready to leave, not just yet. He takes out his tobacco and rolls a smoke and looks out across the valley to Monte Rosa, glowing in the morning sun.

'Bloody beautiful, isn't it?' he says to no one in particular. He then stubs the cigarette out in the ice and stands up shakily, wiping the snow from his clothes.

'Come on. Let's get out of here!' He and his mates turn and cross the ridge into Switzerland, descending in single file.

I edged my way around to the other side of the plinth and looked down into Switzerland. The granite slab dropped into the Saastal, which looked strangely neater, more orderly, than the southern, Italian side. It was empty, no sign of life at all, not a single tree. The bare slopes of the valley converged on a long, narrow lake. It had the same milky, emerald-green water as the Lake of the Fairies in Quarazza. The far end of the valley was closed by the ice-covered summits of central Switzerland.

What I saw on this side was also very different from what Carl saw. In 1943, the glaciers came a long way down towards the stream, and there was no lake. This was created in the 1960s to generate hydroelectricity, submerging the Hotel Mattmart, a four-storey ski resort, which had been there for nearly one hundred years.

A small trail, still visible, unravelled down into the vast valley, skirting around the edge of the lake and disappearing out of view. As they walked down this trail, on the afternoon of 3 October 1943, Carl and his friends were met by English-speaking Swiss guards who escorted them down to the Hotel Mattmart, which had been appropriated as the border control. Here, they were given cigarettes and a hot meal.

Carl Carrigan, his brother Paul Carrigan, Lloyd Ledingham and Ron Fitzgerald – four mates from Moree on the flat plains of northern New South Wales who had signed up together in Moore Park in Sydney three and a half years earlier – were then walked down to the town of Saasfee at the end of the valley, free men at last.

Madonna della Neve, Passo di Monte Moro,
marking the border between Italy and Switzerland.

CHAPTER 9

Over 380 Australian POWs and over one hundred Kiwi POWs made it across the Passo di Monte Moro, and the neighbouring Passo Mondelli, before the bitter winter conditions in 1943 made the crossing virtually impossible, although some did manage to negotiate the appalling conditions.

Battle-hardened New Zealander Laurie Read, who had survived German bayonet charges and getting caught in friendly fire, described his night-time descent into the Saastal, over glaciers and waist-deep snow, as the worst four hours he had ever experienced, including battle action.

By the end of March 1944, the German garrison in Macugnaga had reinforced the border patrols and this escape route was effectively closed.

Although the soldiers were safe, life in Switzerland at the end of 1943 was not easy. The land-locked country was completely surrounded by Axis powers: Germany to the north, Austria to the east, Vichy France to the west and Fascist Italy to the south. Its trade was blockaded by both the Allies and the Axis powers, neither block wanting Switzerland to trade with the other. Germany denounced Switzerland as a medieval remnant and its people as renegade Germans and, under the pan-Germanist Neuordnung doctrine, the German military command had detailed invasion plans drawn up, known as Operation Tannenbaum.

The Swiss were very aware of the danger and their response was to fully mobilise their army and to develop a carrot and stick strategy which they hoped would keep the Germans at bay. They reinforced their border fortification and developed the National Redoubt strategy, which involved abandoning the heavily populated, but very vulnerable, low-lying country and making a stand in the impenetrable High Alps. The idea was to let Germany know that an invasion would come at a very high cost. Simultaneously, as a sweetener, economic concessions were made to Germany in the hope that the overall cost of a German invasion would be perceived to be higher than the potential benefits. At the end of 1943, Hitler still intended to invade Switzerland.

Despite a declaration from a Swiss official in 1938 that 'our little lifeboat is full', the Swiss continued to provide asylum to thousands of people escaping German persecution. They were particularly generous with Allied servicemen who sought refuge during the war. The *évadés* where treated well.

Once Carl made it to Switzerland, his trajectory followed that of the other Allied escapees. He was processed at Saas Fee, fed well, given a fresh set of clothes (British battle dress) and then put on a train to a camp near Zurich. Although the camp was surveilled by Swiss soldiers, it was light-handed. The men were issued with Swiss identity cards and were able to move freely around the towns and surrounding district. They were also able to work in jobs as diverse as forestry workers, farmhands, peat-diggers and even watchmakers. Having had a lifelong passion for horses, Carl found a job as a farrier, shoeing horses, and earning six francs a day.

Notwithstanding initial concerns, the soldiers were received well by the communities they lived amongst, relations were good, and their presence was something of a boon to the towns' struggling economies. This was particularly true of the mountain tourist towns where some of the luckier soldiers were accommodated in disused hotels. Both the Swiss and Allied authorities were mindful of keeping the troops fit and busy so in the winter many of them were given skiing lessons, some becoming proficient enough to take on the locals in downhill skiing competitions. Romances ensued and some of the soldiers brought home Swiss wives.

Even though life was good in Switzerland, most of the soldiers were bored and restless and felt that they were just marking time. Most were very keen to either return home or to get back into action. By mid-1944, the tide of the war had turned. D-Day occurred on 6 June. On 25 August Free French troops liberated Paris, and the following day Marseille was liberated. The French borders opened up, and plans for the repatriation of the soldiers in Switzerland were put into place.

Carl's turn came in September. He left Zurich by train for Marseille and then by ship to Naples. He was shocked by the destruction that both these port cities had suffered from bombing from both the Allies and the Germans. In 1946, my father was also shocked by what he saw in Naples when the London-bound ship my parents were on berthed in the city to offload Italian soldiers who had been POWs in Australia. He said watching the columns of men in their burgundy overcoats marching from the port into the ruins of Naples was one of the saddest things he'd ever seen.

Carl changed ships in Bombay, boarding the US troop carrier *General AE Anderson*. It was a no-frills 'Liberty' ship, built at great speed and with great economy. Carl complained about the lack of comforts and having to sleep on the deck but was full of praise for the American crew who went out of their way to keep the soldiers entertained, including providing board games, table tennis and movies. Carl, and over 400 other members of the AIF, arrived in Melbourne on 17 November 1944. That night, a celebratory dinner was provided for the ex-POWs by General Thomas Blamey, the commander-in-chief of the Australian Military Forces.

The soldiers were sent home within days of their arrival in Melbourne. Carl returned to the family farm in Moree, northern New South Wales. He married and bought his own sheep property on the Queensland–New South Wales border in 1949. He and his wife Marea had ten children before moving to Armidale in the New South Wales tablelands in 1965 so their children could attend local schools and not have to go to boarding school. Carl died on 26 April 1989, aged seventy-six. Although he rarely, and reluctantly, talked about his experiences in Africa and Europe, his wartime colleagues remained close and loyal friends all of his life and Anzac Day on 25 April was always a very special day for him.

Not all the soldiers were so lucky. Grief counselling and post-traumatic stress weren't a thing in 1946. Life had been hard for this generation, particularly country people, growing up in the Great Depression and then being forced to go to war. Loss and tragedy were dealt with stoically. Better not to dwell on things, they were told. Put it behind you and move on. Look to the future. For some this approach worked, for others it didn't. Many suffered depression, which led to alcohol abuse and violence. A study conducted by the

Heidelberg Repatriation Hospital in Melbourne almost fifty years after the end of World War II found that nearly 50 per cent of the veterans interviewed still suffered significant post-traumatic disorder as a result of their combat and prison experiences during the war.

I caught the cable-car back down to Macugnaga. I was tired but relaxed. My mission had been accomplished. Back in my room in the hotel, I had a long conversation on the phone with Carolyn before going out to dinner, this time in the Senner Pub, a micro-brewery in a cellar off the main square, a cosy place down a long flight of stairs. It was lined with timber and black-and-white photos of Alpine landscapes. It had a long bar, with a row of stools on one side and a proud line-up of fifteen spigots on the other, displaying fifteen different types of beer. It was early and I was the only client there.

'*Buona sera*,' said a large young man with a full square beard, who stood on the inside of the bar. '*Benvenuto.*'

'*Buona sera*,' I replied. 'Nice place.'

'*Grazie.* Now, what can I get you?' he said, waving his hand down the line of beer taps.

'What can you suggest? Something local?'

'Well,' he said tapping two of the spigots, 'how about

Balabiot, it's made in Domodossola. You can have a pale ale or a *sciura*, which is a kind of red beer.' He reached a glass and squirted me a taste of the *sciura*.

'You know what? I'm not a big fan of red beer. I think I'll go for the pale ale. A big one please.'

He placed a tall, icy glass of golden beer topped with a collar of creamy white foam in front of me. 'What brings you to Macugnaga at this time of year, if I may ask?'

I had a long draught of the beer, placed it carefully back on the counter. 'I am celebrating having hiked 100 kilometres from Biella to the Passo di Monte Moro.'

'Bravo,' he said, shaking my hand. 'Why did you do that?'

I took another sip of my beer and told him the story, this time the Uncle John version.

'*Pensa te?*' he asked when I had finished. 'My grandfather was a *contrabbandiere*.' He looked quickly around the pub and then leant forward, lowering his voice. 'Don't tell anyone but I think some of the money that went into this pub might have had its origins in smuggling,' He laughed, leant back and asked more seriously, 'You know it's still going on?'

'What's still going on?' I replied.

'Smuggling people over the border. As you would no doubt know,' he added, 'there are a lot of migrants arriving in Italy every year, I think around 200,000 last year. They are mostly young men and young families coming across in leaky boats from Libya, generally landing in Lampedusa off Sicily. Most of them don't want to be in Italy. Why would you? They end up working in tomato-canning factories around Naples earning nothing or selling umbrellas in Milan. Lots of them want to go to France or Germany where the real money is but how to get there? So they run the border.

'There is a little town called Bardonecchia, in the Susa Valley, west of Turin, not so far from here. It seems to be a bit of a hot spot. They can set out from there and cross the Colle della Scala, which I think is about 2000 metres high.'

'Gawd,' I replied, thinking of my own recent experiences. 'That would be very tough.'

'Sure,' he said. 'It takes around six hours, if they are lucky. Poor bastards. I don't think they have any proper gear, a bit like your POWs. The French border guards have snowmobiles, so the migrants take the smaller, higher trails and travel at night. The riskier it is, the safer they feel but I don't think it always works.

'I think around a hundred people have died trying to make the crossing in the last four or five years. I think there are now some groups active in the area who try to help them. You know, give them directions and maybe some better gear and food. Not exactly *passatori* like we had around here but, you know, not that different in some respects. It makes you think, doesn't it?'

I had to agree. 'It sucks, doesn't it?'

He shook his head and wiped down the counter. 'On a

lighter note,' he said, passing me a menu, 'would you like a burger or a burger?'

The next morning I was on the 8.33 commuter bus, white-knuckled, as it travelled at speed down the narrow Anzasca Valley, heading for Domodossola. The steepled slopes of the valley rose sharply on either side, the Anza River roaring in a gully down below me on my right. The driver beeped his horn regularly as he negotiated the blind corners and somehow managed to squeeze the bus through the middle of ancient villages along roads that had been designed for horse-drawn carriages and bicycles. I arrived an hour later in the forecourt of the railway station at Domodossola, the Dome of the Ossola River, a fine town at the foot of the Simplon Pass, which was the home of Elsa Oliva and, in June 1944, was the capital of the short-lived Partisan Republic of the Ossola.

From Domodossola, I caught a train that galloped past the shores of Lake Maggiore, across the plains of the Po Valley, through the dormitory suburbs of Milan before pulling into the arching womb that is Milano Centrale railway station. I got off the train and pulled my bag upstream along the platform, fighting a tide of travellers who were pushing past me to get on the train before it headed back to Domodossola.

I clicked through a turnstile, walked across the concourse and into the safety of Bistrot Centrale, and, in so doing, I completed a 370-kilometre loop that had started in this exact spot ten days earlier. Although it was still morning, I was in a celebratory mood so I ordered a Campari Spritz, sat at a table outside and watched the world go by.

I had planned to stay with Marco and Cristina, my best friends in Milan, but they were down the coast for a week's holiday. They had, however, very generously offered their apartment to me, which was a real treat.

Rather than take a taxi and risk ruining my budget, I took the Metropolitana to Piazza Sant'Ambrogio, then dragged my bags down Via de Amicis to Porta Ticinese. My friends had left the keys to their apartment downstairs with the concierge, a large, friendly lady who occupied a small, windowless office at the entrance to the building. She handed me the keys and a sealed envelope. I thanked her and walked up a flight of stairs, pushed a button and waited as the tiny, caged lift rattled down to the ground floor. I manipulated my way into the cramped space, positioning my luggage so I could close the doors, then pushed button number 4 and I waited with trepidation as the lift rose into the darkness. I got out on the fourth floor, closed the doors and stood on the landing in front of the apartment. I opened the envelope and carefully studied its contents in the half-light: the complicated instructions about how to get through their front door, cross the vestibule and disarm the alarm system. I had fifteen seconds to complete the operation before a siren went off and armed guards were dispatched from a nearby security centre. No margin for error.

Marco's grandfather had been a celebrated painter, sculptor and teacher and one of the founders of the Futurist movement, the most influential artistic movement in Italy in the twentieth century. The walls of the two-floored apartment were covered with magnificent oil paintings and etchings, both by him and his contemporaries. I was very much looking forward to chilling out here for a couple of days before flying home.

The apartment was a short walk from the Navigli, the canal district, where I had been living when I met Marco and Cristina in the 1980s. Much had changed since then, not just in the Navigli, but in most of the city. Milan had gone from being a provincial city on the rise to being a full-blown metropolis. Back in the day, the Navigli had been a rough area: a working-class suburb haunted by petty criminals, large families from the south struggling to get a foothold in the booming industrial city, some bohemians and a few foreigners. These days, the Navigli is pumping most evenings, filled with the gilded youth of the city. The canals are lined with ropes of fairy-lights and the footpaths are crowded with tables spilling out of fashionable cafes and expensive restaurants.

I was very happy to first go down to the small supermarket on the ground floor of the building, stock up and then return to the apartment, kick off my boots and stay indoors. I spent most of my time downstairs in the large kitchen, grazing, scribbling notes in my exercise book and reflecting on my adventure crossing the Alps.

Although I had promised myself I would never do it again, after my shoulders had stopped aching and my feet had stopped throbbing, and I realised that I had loved the experience, I began planning how I could squeeze in the hike again next year. It had been a grand adventure.

Grinding my way over those mountains, I had developed a passion for the gnarly, indomitable western Alps. I was in awe of the immensity of those ancient ranges. I had also acquired a great affection for the gruff *montanari*, the people who inhabit the western Alps, reserved people who are quick to laugh, offer hospitality and help. I had even picked up a taste for their stodgy food: those salamis, as gnarly as the mountains themselves; the soupy polenta; the hard cheeses and thick stews; and the rough red wines and burning grappa.

I had also become fascinated by the stories that revealed themselves as I hiked those stony trails and wanted to learn more about them: the creation stories about the collision of tectonic plates and the descent and retreat of great rivers of ice; the tales of the cussed medieval migrants who crossed mountains and glaciers to settle and thrive in empty places that no one else could reach; and the dramas of the twentieth century: the heroes and the villains, the Fascists and the partisans, the Jewish refugees and the Anzac escapees who were so out of place in these godless mountains.

Perhaps most importantly, I had developed a much deeper understanding of, and respect for, the young men, including Carl Carrigan, my uncle John and my father, who had volunteered to fight on foreign shores, to confront unmitigated evil, to put their lives on the line in the name of country, empire and the future: their future and the future of their children. I now appreciated that the peace and prosperity that I have enjoyed throughout my life is, in a large part, thanks to them and the sacrifices that they made during those years.

It is believed that 9572 young Australians died in Europe during World War II, and one of them was my uncle John Tancred. Lives cut short. John had been a significant part of my growing up, an inspiration and a source of comfort when I was little. I really did feel that his sacrifice deserved far more than a watery grave and an inscription on a stone column in the middle of the Libyan desert. This is true of the many millions of other young people whose lives were also cut short, unfulfilled. Anonymous. Uncle John as Everyman, as the Universal Soldier? I liked that. I hoped that by doing the hike and by researching and recording something of his life, I had given him the recognition and respect he deserved but had perhaps never received. Like so many, John was a decent and brave person caught up in a brutal war who merited this, at the very least.

AFTERWORD

I have been back many times to that corner of Italy and the western Alps since that first hike in 2013. Mostly leading hikes. I took the first group on the Trails to Freedom hike in 2015. It included three of Carl Carrigan's daughters: Belinda, Jane and Carmel. The children of other escapees have joined me on later tours. It is always a moving experience, especially when we get to the Swiss border and look down into the Saas Valley.

Our regular visits have also awoken the interest of the locals, reminding them of a chapter in their history that has often been forgotten. This is particularly true of Macugnaga, the town at the end of the hike on the Swiss border, where the presence of a group of Australians, packs on their backs, coming down from the Quarazza Valley at the end of each summer, has helped revive interest in their own history, in which they take great pride: smugglers-turned-rescuers who saved over 500 people's lives.

On 29 August 2024, in conjunction with the municipality of Macugnaga, the Club Alpinista Italiana (CAI), the local *Il Rosa* newspaper and Hidden Italy, a plaque was installed on the plinth of the statue of the Madonna delle Neve which stands on the Italian–Swiss border, exactly where Carl Carrigan, Paul Carrigan, Ron Fitzgerald and Lloyd Ledingham crossed to safety, eighty years earlier. The plaque reads:

80 years after the ANZAC soldiers' last crossing, with this plaque we commemorate the many Italians putting themselves and their families at risk, between 1943 and 1944, who helped over 500 hundred young Australians and New Zealanders escape the grip of Fascism and reach freedom in Switzerland.

A 80 anni dagli ultimi passaggi dei soldati ANZAC, con questa targa commemmoriamo i tanti italiani che, mettendo a repentaglio se stessi e le loro famiglie, tra il 1943 e il 1944, hanno aiutato oltre 500 giovani australiani e neozelandesi a raggiugere la liberta in Svizzzera, sfuggendo cosi alla morsa del fascismo.

Macugnaga - Monte Rosa

"80 years after the ANZAC soldiers' last crossing, with this plaque we commemorate the many Italians who, putting themselves and their families at risk, between 1943 and 1944, helped over 500 young Australians and New Zealanders escape the grip of fascism and reach freedom in Switzerland."

"A 80 anni dagli ultimi passaggi dei soldati ANZAC, con questa targa commemoriamo i tanti italiani che, mettendo a repentaglio sé stessi e le loro famiglie, tra il 1943 e il 1944, hanno aiutato oltre 500 giovani australiani e neozelandesi a raggiungere la libertà in Svizzera, sfuggendo così alla morsa del fascismo."

Macugnaga, 27 agosto 2024

ACKNOWLEDGEMENTS

I'd like to thank Cate Carrigan for bringing me her father Carl's story and, with the rest of her family, for allowing me to share it; Dr Kate Kittel and her marvellous research (*Shooting Through*) which brought this extraordinary historical episode to life; Stuart McDonald for his sage advice and encouragement; Tom Gilliat and the team at Hardie Grant; Dr Elizabeth Tancred, my big sister, for her unwavering support; my errant brother Tony; and our guides in Piedmont, Dr Matteo Negro, Giorgio Farinetti and Diletta Zanetti.

I'd also like to thank Carolyn O'Donnell, the love of my life, for her tolerance, forbearance and love; as well as Grace and Peter, for turning out to be such wonderful people.

READING LIST

GENERAL

Stefano Ardito, *Grandi Sentieri d'Italia* (Great Italian Paths), 1987.

Robert Byron, *The Road to Oxiana*, 1937.

Paolo Cognetti, *Le Otto Montagne* (The Eight Mountains), 2016.

Roger Deakin, *Waterlog*, 1999.

Robert Macfarlane, *The Old Ways: A Journey on Foot*, 2012.

Louis Oreiller con Irene Borgna, *Il Pastore di Stambecchi: Storia di una vita fuori traccia* (The Shepherd of Ibex: Story of a life without traces), 2018.

Mario Rigoni Stern, *Amore di Confine* (Border Love), 1986.

TRAILS TO FREEDOM

Anna Maria Accati, *Infanzia di Guerra in Valle Cervo: Un giardino di ricordi* (Childhood at War in the Valle Cervo: A garden of memories), 2014.

Alberto Anzani, *Sul Confine* (On the Border), 2004.

Giorgio Bocca, *Storia dell'Italia Partigiana: Settembre 1943–Maggio 1945*, (The History of Partisan Italy: September 1943–May 1945), 1966.

RJB Bosworth, *Mussolini*, 2002.

Cate Carrigan, *Italy to the Alps: A Wartime Odyssey*, 2019 (revised).

Beppe Fenoglio, *Partigiano Johnny* (Johnny the Partisan), 1968.

Edgardo Ferrari, *La Repubblica dell'Ossola, una guida alla storia ed ai luoghi* (The Republic of the Ossola Valley, a guide to the history and places), 2001.

Paul Ginsborg, *A History of Contemporary Italy*, 1990.

Susan Jacobs, *Fighting with the Enemy: New Zealand POWs and the Italian Resistance*, 2003.

Katrina Kittel, *Shooting Through: Campo 106 escaped POWs after the Italian Armistice*, 2019.

Primo Levi, *Il Sistema Periodico* (The Periodic Table), 1975.

Sergio Luzzatto, *Partigia* (Primo Levi's Resistance), 2013.

Elsa Oliva, *Ragazza Partigiana* (The Girl Partisan), 1969.

Elsa Oliva, *La Repubblica Partigiana dell'Ossola* (The Partisan Republic of the Ossola Valley), 1983.

Enrico Pagano (editor), *L'Impegno, revisita semestrale del Istituto per la Storia della Resistenza, Varallo* (L'Impegno, the bi-annual review of the Institute for the History of the Resistance, Varallo).

Touring Club Italiano, *Piemonte* (Regional Guide), 2006.

Stuart Woolf (ed), *The Rebirth of Italy, 1943–1950*, 1972.